A Compassionate Heart

The CAFOD/DLT Lent Book 2003

Clare Amos ♦ Tina Beattie
Joan Chittister ♦ Joseph Donders
Beverley McAinsh ♦ Michael Nuttall

A Compassionate Heart

Reflections on the
Scripture Readings for Lent 2003

CAFOD — IT'S TIME FOR JUSTICE

DARTON·LONGMAN+TODD

First published in Great Britain in 2002 by

CAFOD
Romero Close
Stockwell Road
London SW9 9TY

Darton, Longman and Todd Ltd
1 Spencer Court
140-142 Wandsworth High Street
London SW18 4JJ

© 2002 Clare Amos, Tina Beattie, Joan Chittister,
Joseph Donders, Beverley McAinsh, Michael Nuttall

ISBN 0 232 52480 7

The right of Clare Amos, Tina Beattie, Joan Chittister,
Joseph Donders, Beverley McAinsh and Michael Nuttall
to be identified as authors of this work has been
asserted in accordance with the Copyright,
Designs and Patents Act 1988.

Cover photo: Simon Rawles
Design: Garry Lambert

Bible quotations are taken from the New Jerusalem Bible,
published and copyright (c) 1985 by Darton, Longman and
Todd Ltd and Doubleday, a division of Random House, Inc.

Printed and bound in Great Britain by Page Bros,
Norwich, Norfolk

Contents

Introducing CAFOD — vi

About the authors — vii

Introduction — ix

Ash Wednesday to Saturday after Ash Wednesday	*Tina Beattie*	2
First week of Lent	*Tina Beattie*	10
Second week of Lent	*Beverley McAinsh*	24
Third week of Lent	*Joseph Donders*	38
Fourth week of Lent	*Joan Chittister*	52
Fifth week of Lent	*Michael Nuttall*	66
Holy Week	*Clare Amos*	80

Introducing CAFOD

CAFOD is a major British charity that works in partnership with some of the world's poorest communities to address the causes of underdevelopment. It also responds to the needs of people affected by emergencies such as war and natural disaster, raises awareness of the causes of third world poverty and campaigns for change.

CAFOD believes that all human beings have a right to dignity and respect and that the world's resources are a gift to be shared by all men and women, whatever their race, nationality or religion.

CAFOD is the English and Welsh arm of Caritas Internationalis, a worldwide network of Catholic relief and development organisations.

About the authors

Clare Amos is Theological Resource Officer of the Anglican world mission agency USPG and honorary editor of *The Reader*, the national magazine for Anglican Readers.

Tina Beattie is a lecturer in Christianity at Digby Stuart College at the University of Surrey, Roehampton. She has written widely on Catholic theology and women's spirituality.

Joan Chittister is a member and former prioress of the Benedictine sisters of Erie, Pennsylvania. Her many books include *The Story of Ruth: Twelve Moments in Every Woman's Life*.

Joseph Donders teaches and lectures worldwide. His many books include *Praying and Preaching the Sunday Gospel* and *The Fullness of Time*.

Beverley McAinsh is Director of the Living Spirituality Network and the Producer of "Something Understood", the weekly spiritual anthology broadcast on BBC Radio 4.

Michael Nuttall was the Anglican Bishop of Natal, South Africa from 1982-2000. He was known in the final years of the apartheid era as "Number Two to Tutu".

Introduction

Lent is a time when Christians try to narrow the gap between the way shown to us in the scriptures and the real path that our lives are taking.

We tend to make our faith a private matter, to put spirituality into a different category to the 'real world' of work and taxes and politics and wars.

Yet as one writer in these reflections reminds us, the 'real' world is one in which the cost of providing food and medical care for all the sick and hungry children of the world for a year can be spent on the purchase of three aircraft carriers. It is estimated that on *each day* of Lent this year over 20,000 children will die from hunger and preventable diseases such as diarrhoea and measles.

This is a reality that has lost touch with the truth about humanity, the reality of our common inheritance as children of God.

In *A Compassionate Heart* six writers show that the call of the gospel is to more than a life of private prayer, to more than the correct observance of rules and rituals. It invites a personal transformation, a new way of seeing, the discovery of a compassionate heart. As Joan Chittister writes, in Lent 'we try to live our life as God shows us: oozing generosity, just in all our ways, bringers of beauty, promoters of life and always open to new possibilities'.

'The scriptures are clear,' another contributor writes, 'these readings are not about another people in another world. It is we who must sit up and listen to the messengers God is sending us.'

A Compassionate Heart

The CAFOD/DLT Lent Book 2003

Tina Beattie

Ash Wednesday to Saturday after Ash Wednesday

Ash Wednesday

Hunger, repentance and solidarity

Jl 2:12-18; Ps 50:3-6, 12-14, 17; 2 Cor 5:20-6:2; Mt 6:1-6, 16-18

"Order a fast, proclaim a solemn assembly, call the people together, summon the community."

(Joel 2:15-16)

Many Christians argue that giving things up for Lent is spiritually misguided, since the Christian way of life should continually be one of prayerful self-discipline. Others, myself included, value at least in principle the ancient tradition of abstinence and alms-giving, even if we weaken at the first temptation. My own Lenten failures are a family joke.

Today, most western Christians are more affluent than ever before, yet we are less committed than we have ever been to spiritual practices of fasting and abstinence. Perhaps we need to rediscover the holiness of Lenten sacrifice, a holiness that invites us to reflect upon our weakness and sinfulness but also to celebrate our potential for wholeness: the wholeness of body and spirit and the wholeness and interdependence of our human community made up of rich and poor, young and old, women and men. Joel envisages such a community, gathered together in fasting and repentance, responding to the gracious invitation of a tender and compassionate God.

Christianity is a faith not of spiritual abstractions but of incarnation, of bodiliness. As creatures, we are dependent on the earth and participate in the cycles of nature. By observing the fasts and feasts of the liturgical year we make a living sacrament out of our bodies, sharing in the life of the body of the Church in our physical needs as well as in our worship and prayers. Fasting can be an expression of community that makes us aware of that collective body and those within it for whom hunger and thirst are a way of life. The Indian theologian Aloysius Pieris makes a distinction between voluntary poverty as a Christian vocation, and enforced poverty as a social evil. When we voluntarily forego some of the privileges of our affluent society we express our solidarity with the poor and our protest against the evil of enforced poverty in a world of plenty.

The purpose of fasting and alms-giving is both a physical expression of being one body with those who suffer and a spiritual exercise. In the hunger and weakness of our bodies we come to understand our poverty and need before God, our broken-heartedness, and our dependence on the graciousness of our tender and compassionate Lord.

Thought for the day

The average citizen of an industrial nation consumes 40 per cent more than the UN recommended daily intake of 2,350 calories per day, while the average third world resident consumes ten per cent less than the recommended daily intake.

Prayer

God of the hungry; tender and compassionate God, forgive us for our greed and our indifference to those in need. Strengthen us and guide us to hear your call and return to you, so that in Christ we too might become 'the goodness of God' in our suffering world.

Amen

Thursday after Ash Wednesday
Forgiveness and the fullness of life
Dt 30:15-20; Ps 1:1-4, 6; Lk 9:22-25

"If anyone wants to be a follower of mine, let them renounce themselves and take up their cross every day and follow me."

(Luke 9:23)

The idea of bearing one's cross is often used to justify a dismal kind of spirituality, in which following Christ means accepting avoidable suffering and abuse in the hope that things will be better in heaven. This is the kind of religion that Marx referred to as "the opium of the people". It does not inspire the oppressed to rise up against injustice, but rather persuades them that oppression is a cross that Christ wants them to bear, that Christian renunciation of self calls for passivity in the face of exploitation. Women in particular have been encouraged to model their spirituality on this kind of self-martyrdom, so that their own identity becomes swallowed up in the demands and expectations of others.

Irenaeus said that "the glory of God is a person fully alive." Jesus does not speak of passive suffering, but of an active daily commitment to follow him. What does the cross mean in this context? It is an awesome symbol, because it calls for a giving over of one's whole being to God out of love for those who suffer the torments and injustices of our sinful world. Many Christians have been called to share in Christ's death as an expression of such love. But for most of us, following Christ feels like a less dramatic and perhaps a less committed struggle. Whatever our calling, however, taking up our cross means actively seeking to become the person we are called to be, refusing to lose ourselves amidst the false promises and deceptive rewards of our consumerist culture, and patterning ourselves on Christ in order to be fully alive.

We can be encouraged in this, even when we fail, by remembering that the cross is first and foremost a symbol of forgiveness and new life. It is the tree of life, where we find rebirth out of failure, death and suffering. The person who takes up his or her cross is "like a tree that is planted beside the flowing waters", a person fully alive, a person who, faced with "life or death, blessing or curse", says 'Yes' to the blessing of life in all its tragedy and joy.

Thought for the day

We cannot do everything, and there is a sense of liberation in realising that. This enables us to do something, and to do it very well. It may be incomplete, but it is a beginning, a step along the way, an opportunity for the Lord's grace to enter and do the rest. (Oscar Romero)

Prayer

Jesus Christ, you offer us the fullness of life. Help us to follow you, so that your cross might become a tree of life that brings wholeness and healing to our divided and suffering world.

Amen

Friday after Ash Wednesday
Religious ritual and social injustice

Is 58:1-9; Ps 51:3-6, 18-19; Mt 9:14-15

"Is not this the sort of fast that pleases me – it is the Lord who speaks – to break unjust fetters and undo the thongs of the yoke?"

(Isaiah 58)

Today's readings remind us that Christianity shares with Judaism an ancient suspicion of so-called "religion". God does not want ostentatious religiosity or flamboyant displays of devotion. Indeed, all our religious observances count for less than nothing without justice and love for the poor. The first Christians were often accused of atheism by their Greek and Roman neighbours, because they took no part in the religious festivities of the Roman empire. They saw, more clearly perhaps than we do today, that the Gospel message was one of radical freedom – from the tyranny and caprice of the ancient gods, from the humiliation of religious practices that enslaved the human spirit, and from a society in which slaves, women, children and the poor counted for nothing. A second century letter, the Epistle to Diognetus, says of the early Christians, "They are poor, and make many rich; they lack everything, and in everything they abound." Of course, we know that the early Church had its share of conflict, and it's not hard to detect a bit of spin-doctoring in that letter. But it tells us something about a vision that those Christians aspired to, even if they didn't always live up to it.

Today, at least in the western democracies, the Church is not a marginalised and persecuted community. Even in our secular era, Christian institutions wield considerable power in society. Isaiah's call is not to the pious individual nor even to devout communities – it is a call to the nation. It is predominantly Christian nations that wield the greatest military, economic and political power in the modern world, and Christians are therefore complicit in the injustice, inequality and violence of that world. Next time we see the lavish ceremonials of church and state on our television screens perhaps we ought to listen for the voice of Isaiah, reminding us that our religious rituals alienate us from God unless they are motivated by an active and passionate commitment to "let the oppressed go free, and break every yoke, to share your bread with the hungry, and shelter the homeless poor."

Thought for the day

What is the use of loading Christ's table with gold cups while he himself is starving? Feed the hungry and then if you have any money left over, spend it on the altar table.

(St John Chrysostom)

Prayer

God of justice, give us the strength to be different, so that we are recognised not by the extravagance of our rituals, but by our love for one another and for the poor and vulnerable.

Amen

Saturday after Ash Wednesday
The man who came to dinner
Is 58:9-14; Ps 85:1-6; Lk 5:27-32

"The Pharisees and their scribes complained to his disciples and said, 'Why do you eat and drink with tax collectors and sinners?' Jesus said to them in reply, 'It is not those who are well who need the doctor, but the sick.'"

(Luke 5:30-31)

In today's first reading Isaiah's voice cries a warning to our complacent and affluent culture. Justice to the poor and refraining from doing business on the Sabbath go hand in hand. Happiness lies in balanced lives where justice and worship, work and rest, go hand in hand, not in the seven-day-a-week frenzy that drives the "haves" in our society, while a growing number of "have-nots" are pushed further and further to the margins. We are a sick society. But Jesus says that he has come, not to the virtuous but to sinners, not to those who are well but to those who are sick.

In this warped culture, "spirituality" has become part of a personal fitness agenda, along with going to the gym and counting calories. We are all familiar with the benign smile – perhaps we use it ourselves – that goes with the words, "I'm not religious, I'm spiritual." I don't think Levi the tax collector was spiritual, and he probably wasn't religious either, judging by the attitudes of the religious leaders. But Jesus feasted at his house, to the disapproval of those who were known for their spirituality and religiosity. The behaviour of Jesus reminds us that God is not impressed by our achievements and our social status, nor by our religious and spiritual credentials. God simply wants us to pause for long enough to hear the words "follow me", to find time to say with sincere and contrite hearts, "Turn your ear, O Lord, and give answer for I am poor and needy." Then he will come and eat with us, in the presence of the friends and strangers we welcome into our homes.

But would we risk such a house guest? Jesus enjoyed the company of tax collectors, sinners and prostitutes. He frequently caused offence. Perhaps he was bored by conversations about the ancient equivalents of interest rates, property prices and summer holidays. Too often we mistake politeness and conformity for goodness. Real goodness is gutsy, honest and not overly concerned with manners and social niceties.

Thought for the day
Was Jesus the kind of person I would invite to dinner?

Prayer
God, help us to see you among those whom society and religion reject. Open our eyes to all that is false and pretentious around us, and teach us to cherish the good in the outcasts and prostitutes you chose to befriend.

Amen

Tina Beattie

First week of Lent

First Sunday of Lent

A rainbow-coloured promise

Gen 9:8-15; Ps 24:4-9; 1 Pet 3:18-22; Mk 1:12-15

"No thing of flesh shall be swept away again by the waters of the flood. There shall be no flood to destroy the earth again."

(Genesis 9:11)

Sometimes, there seems to be a gulf between the promises of the Bible and the realities of our world. In recent years we have seen devastating floods in countries such as Bangladesh, Mozambique, Honduras and Nicaragua. Whatever the complex reasons for these environmental disasters, they are not simply "acts of God". Global warming and deforestation are major contributory factors. It is the greed of the rich that wreaks such devastation on the lives of the poor.

St Peter tells us that the flood waters are symbolic of baptism. To discern their real meaning we must focus our attention on the risen Christ and know that in him we are eternally safe. But symbolic meanings are dangerous if they foster in us an escapist spirituality that is not concerned with the realities of the world around us. There is a line in a poem by Roger McGough that reads, "A drowning surrealist will not appreciate the concrete lifebelt." Christian spirituality is surreal if it blinds us to the urgency and avoidability of much human suffering, and our language about love and redemption is little more than a concrete lifebelt thrown to the drowning unless it is accompanied by an active commitment to work for justice.

If we believe in the resurrection, if we believe that in Christ there is no power on heaven or earth great enough to destroy us, then we will see beyond the panic-driven and nihilistic greed of those who think this life is the only chance they have to succeed, to prosper and to consume. Genesis speaks of God's Covenant. A Covenant is a two-way promise. When we accept God's promise to us in Christ, we reciprocate by agreeing to share God's vision for life on earth as well as in heaven. Free from the pressures of materialism, confident of our eternal well-being, we find the hope and the long-term vision we need if we are to build societies where "all things of the flesh" live in the generosity and abundance of our creator. We begin to share God's rainbow-coloured dream of justice, peace and freedom from fear, allowing it to suffuse our human endeavours and encounters from our most intimate relationships to our global economy.

Thought for the day

God dreams for us. Today, at this moment, God has an image and a hope for what we are becoming. We should not let God dream alone. (Dorothee Solle)

Prayer

Lord God, the rainbow reveals to us the beauty of your promise. May our world become a rainbow-coloured family where all your people live together in a peace that foretells of our eternal peace with you.

Amen

First Monday of Lent

How to be happy

Lev 19:1-2, 11-18; Ps 18:8-10, 15; Mt 25:31-46

*"The precepts of the Lord are right,
they gladden the heart.
The command of the Lord is clear,
it gives light to the eyes."*

(Psalm 18:8)

In the pre-modern world, Christian morality was understood not in terms of duty, but in terms of happiness. Thomas Aquinas taught that the good life was also the happy life. It was with thinkers such as Immanuel Kant in the seventeenth century that western concepts of morality changed. Being good was about doing one's duty, not about being happy. Today, many people still see morality as something burdensome, so that we are a culture that tends to contrast being good with being happy, being moral with having fun. It is perhaps not surprising that, in the blind pursuit of happiness, we seem ever more willing to sacrifice goodness.

The journalist Cal McCrystal writes that "happiness is the shadow cast by something else". Happiness itself is an elusive quality. The more we pursue it for its own sake, the more it evades us. The psalmist tells us that following God's laws will bring us happiness, and the readings from Leviticus and Matthew's Gospel tell us what those laws are. They are social laws, grounded in an ethos of care and compassion, integrity and justice. They teach us that if we want to be happy individuals then we must work for the good of society as a whole.

Our society has been seduced by the myth of happiness divorced from goodness and social justice. A recent survey showed that television programmes featuring third world countries are more and more devoted to holidays and shows such as *Survivor*, and less and less to the social realities of those countries. Such escapism will never deliver the happiness it claims to offer, for happiness can only be found in the real world, in a world governed by God's laws of interdependence, community and solicitude.

As western culture moves further and further away from truth and reality, Christians are increasingly at the forefront of work for social justice, whether this has to do with caring for the marginalised in our own society or with campaigning for justice for the world's poorer nations. When such work is motivated, not by an onerous sense of religious duty but by a generous spirit of solidarity, then it is good work, and the shadow which it casts is happiness.

Thought for the day
Happiness is the shadow cast by something else. (Cal McCrystal)

Prayer
God, give us the wisdom to recognise that elusive happiness which we find only in goodness, truth and love.

Amen

First Tuesday of Lent
Prayer and the will of God

Is 55:10-11; Ps 33:4-7, 16-19; Mt 6:7-15

"If you forgive others their failings, your heavenly Father will forgive you yours."

(Matthew 6:14)

Isaiah tells us that God's word achieves what it sets out to do as naturally as the rain waters the earth. This idea of the inevitability of God's will can lead to a tyrannical concept of an omnipotent being who rules with a rod of iron. But the psalmist invites us to a different understanding of God, as one whose will is entirely directed towards the flourishing of humankind. This is a God who frees us from our terrors and makes us radiant, a God who is close to the broken-hearted, and who saves those whose spirits are crushed. It is consoling to know that this compassionate will makes the laws that govern the cosmos.

The readings today also draw us into the mystery and paradox of prayer. God's will cannot be thwarted, but we also have Christ's great teaching on prayer. Surely, prayer is futile unless we believe that we can influence God? But if we attend to what Jesus says about prayer it resonates with the same message as those of the prophet and the psalmist. We do not pray to tell God what we need for God already knows what we need. We pray because we want to share in God's will for the world. In the opening prayer, we ask God to "help us to grow in our desire for you". When we grow in our desire for God, we learn how to desire the justice and joy that God will achieve, with or without our help.

This is a commitment that involves judgement. "The Lord turns his face against the wicked." In standing for some values, we must stand against others. But we are not God, and the choices we make are not always wise. Sometimes we collude in injustice, because that makes our lives more comfortable. At other times, we misjudge situations. In this complex world, there are few absolute rights and wrongs, and the decisions we make are often ambiguous.

That is why our lives must be suffused by a spirit of forgiveness. We fail, and we are surrounded by the failures of others. Through mutual forgiveness, we can be honest about our failings, renewed in our desire for God, faithful in our vision, and restored in our relationships.

Thought for the day
Prayer is learning to sing in tune to the music of God.

Prayer
Lord God, teach us how to pray, so that in prayer we open our whole beings to you and become the living expression of your love for the world.

Amen

First Wednesday in Lent
Justice as a remedy for violence

Jon 3:1-10; Ps 50:3-4, 12-13, 18-19; Lk 11:29-32

"God saw their efforts to renounce their evil behaviour. And God relented: he did not inflict on them the disaster which he had threatened."

(Jonah 3:10)

Some Christians interpreted the catastrophe of 11 September 2001 as a sign of God's punishment, because America had become a godless nation. For many of us such ideas are deeply offensive. Similarly, God's threat to destroy Ninevah does not sit easily with our modern sensibilities. We want God to be a tolerant liberal, like us.

But so-called tolerant liberalism is often neither tolerant nor liberal. Our modern secular democracies shield us from reality. They seduce us into a make-believe world where we never have to confront the people who live on the margins of our own societies, let alone those who live in countries that we visit only as tourists and holidaymakers. They teach us to believe the lie that our security depends on war and militarism, rather than on justice and a fair distribution of the earth's resources.

There is a line in Spike Lee's film, Malcolm X: "The most dangerous person in the world is the person with nothing to lose." Suicide bombers and those who fly planes into buildings are dangerous because they think they have nothing to lose, and they seem to have grown to hate a social order that offers them nothing worth living for.

If we want to enjoy security and peace then we must repent, turn away from injustice, and create a world where everybody has something of value, and therefore everybody has something to lose.

However, God is liberal, if not tolerant. If we choose to carry on as we are God respects our freedom to do so, but we must face the consequences of our choices. There is a difference between an ancient world view that saw all suffering as God's punishment, and a modern world view that recognises the relationship between injustice and violence. But the message is the same: if we want peace, then we must repent and work for justice.

Thought for the day

Whenever I think how hard it is to keep writing about love in these times of tension and strife which may at any moment become for us all a time of terror, I think to myself, "What else is the world interested in? What else do we all want, each one of us, except to love and be loved? Even the most ardent revolutionist is trying to make a world where it is easier for people to love, to stand in that relationship with each other of love." (Dorothy Day, writing in 1948)

Prayer

God, give us the courage to speak truth to power, but teach us to temper truth with gentleness. Give us pure hearts and steadfast spirits, so that we may become people who hear your call to relent, and who turn the world from violence to peace through mending the broken bonds of love and justice.

Amen

First Thursday in Lent

The power and powerlessness of women

Est 4:17; Ps 137:1-3, 7-8; Mt 7:7-12

*"As for ourselves, save us by your hand,
and come to my help, for I am alone
and have no one but you, Lord."*

(Esther 4:17)

Today is one of those rare occasions when a woman's voice rings out from the pages of the Bible. Esther says that she has no helper but God, but she is strengthened by the certainty of God's help and is able to do great things for her people. There are many women like Esther in our world today. Lacking in worldly power, they are empowered by their faith in God, their passion to make a better society for their children, and their sense of solidarity with one another. Sojourner Truth, a freed slave woman in nineteenth century America, said, "If the first woman God ever made was strong enough to turn the world upside down, all alone, together women ought to be able to turn it rightside up again."

It is easy to be preoccupied by the injustices and sufferings of our modern world, so that we sometimes fail to celebrate the goodness of our times. Today, people who have been condemned to silence for much of history are beginning to speak, to tell their stories, to describe their dreams. Women, colonised peoples, indigenous peoples and those of non-western cultures and faiths are finding spaces in which to make their voices heard, telling histories and herstories that we have never heard before. Those of us who have not been challenged in our view of the world are called to stop and listen, to learn, and to change.

"Search, and you will find." People who have been searching through history for a sense of identity and belonging are finding what they were looking for. The shadow side of this is the emergence of many kinds of nationalism and fundamentalism, while at the same time the global order has the power to eradicate these emergent signs of human plurality by subsuming us all within a western-dominated market economy. That is why we need to turn away from the din of the media and the clamour of the markets, and to tune our ears to the lonely voices, the women's voices, the voices that drift from the margins of our social structures, inviting us to share a different vision of how the world might be.

Thought for the day

"Women, in and through their powerlessness, understand what it means to be vulnerable. Their openness to beginnings, even under conditions of hardship and privation, terror and torture, has daily renewed the world, making possible future beginnings. Women, from a double position that straddles powerlessness and power, are in a powerful position to insist with Albert Camus that one must never avert one's eyes from the suffering of children and, seeing that suffering, one is required to act."
(Jean Bethke Elshtain)

Prayer

You stretch out your hand and save me,
your hand will do all things for me.
Your love, O Lord, is eternal,
discard not the work of your hands.

Amen

First Friday in Lent
Confession and reconciliation

Ezek 18:21-28; Ps 129; Mt 5:20-26

"If your virtue goes no deeper than that of the scribes and Pharisees, you will never get into the kingdom of heaven."

(Matthew 5:20)

Jesus calls us to a radical form of peacemaking which asks us to behave in ways that most of us find very difficult. How often do we cover over our resentments and grudges with a tight-lipped smile rather than struggling for words that would help us to acknowledge together our anxieties, fears and insecurities? Jesus does not say that we will never be angry with one another or feel hurt but he does say that reconciliation is the precondition for worship.

The confessional is one way in which Catholics have acknowledged their sins against the community of the Church but for many Christians today traditional concepts of sin no longer offer us a truthful language of confession. The Church's thinking about sin often seems too narrowly focused on issues of sexuality or private morality, and it is not always informed by an awareness of the psychological and social dimensions of sin. Modern communications mean that we are confronted daily by the moral challenges that arise in a world in which the human family seems paradoxically both more interdependent and more divided than ever before. Perhaps in shaping a morality for the future, we need to rediscover the wisdom of the past, when people were more aware of the ways in which they depended upon one another and nature.

The Latin American writer Eduardo Galeano imagines a priest hearing confessions among Mexican Indians, with a translator struggling to communicate to him the mysteries of the sins being confessed. "He says he mistreated the fire. He cursed the flames because they didn't glow brightly. He says he profaned the path, that he cut it back when there was no need. He says he chopped down a tree and he didn't tell it why. ... The priest didn't know what to do with these sins that were not on Moses's list."

We need poets and visionaries to help us to find a new language of sin and reconciliation, so that we can reach out to one another in a shared longing for integrity and peace. Forgiveness is the first step towards the healing of broken relationships and the making of friendship – with one another, with God, and with the natural world.

Thought for the day

"I have a friend who, if I happen to be too busy to take the call, leaves a simple message: 'Tell her I called.' It is enough to dissolve all the cares of the day. According to the teachings of Buddhism a good friend is one who gives things hard to give, does what is hard, bears with hard words, tells you his secrets, guards your secrets assiduously, does not forsake you in times of want and does not condemn you when you are ruined. With such friends, one can travel the roughest road and not be defeated by hardship." (Aung San Suu Kyi)

Prayer

Lord God, teach us how to rediscover the joy of living in community and interdependence, so that our wounded and divided world might be restored to wholeness through our openness to your healing love.

Amen

First Saturday in Lent
What is the real world?
Dt 26:16-19; Ps 118:1-2, 4-5, 7-8; Mt 5:43-48

"You must therefore be perfect just as your heavenly Father is perfect."

(Matthew 5:48)

The Gospel reading today seems impossible in the demands it makes of us. "Love your enemies and pray for those who persecute you." For centuries, there has been a tendency in Christianity to separate the spiritual message of Jesus' teaching from the "real" world of politics and business. Christian ethics became focused on the cultivation of highly individualistic moral and spiritual attributes, while having little to say about wider social issues. The implication is that it's fine to indulge in warm loving feelings in private, but they don't really stand up to the test of reality.

Yet how often do we pause to ask ourselves just how real the so-called "real world" is? Since 11 September 2001 there have been massive increases in military spending in America and Britain, because of what is called the "war on terrorism". These two countries, self-appointed custodians of global peace, also happen to be among the world's major arms manufacturers. In 2001 British arms exports to countries such as Pakistan, Turkey, Saudi Arabia, Indonesia, India and Israel increased dramatically. For the cost of three US Nimitz aircraft carriers, it would be possible to provide food and medical care for all the sick and hungry children of the world for a year. An estimated 32,700 people, 24,000 of them children, die every day from hunger and preventable diseases such as diarrhoea and measles.

Figures such as these are manifestations not of a real world, but of a world in the grip of some dark and violent fantasy that has lost its grip on reality. Jesus' words ring out, not as the spiritual platitudes of a New Age dreamer, but as an urgent and practical call to peace. Compared with the human and economic cost of hating our enemies, Christ's is the voice of reality and reason. It is never too late. The smallest gesture of peace acquires momentous significance, in a world that appears to be fragmenting under the combined forces of hatred, fear and war.

Thought for the Day

"Never before has man had such capacity to control his own destiny, to end thirst and hunger, to conquer poverty and disease, to banish illiteracy and massive human misery. We have the power to make this the best generation in the history of mankind – or make it the last." (John F. Kennedy, Address to the United Nations General Assembly, 20 September 1963)

Prayer

Lord God, set us free from the seductive illusions of violence and war. Give our political leaders the inspiration and courage to work for peace, and help us to turn our scientific and technological genius from the service of death to the service of life.

Amen

Beverley McAinsh

Second week of Lent

Second Sunday of Lent

Beloved

Gen 22:1-2, 9-13, 15-18; Rom 8:31-34; Mk 9:2-10; Ps 115:10, 15-19

"And a cloud came, covering them in shadow; and there came a voice from the cloud, 'This is my Son, the Beloved ...' "

(Mark 9:7-8)

To take a word out of context and use it shamelessly in the service of one's own agenda is the high crime of biblical exegesis. So I confess to the crime, but I don't repent. "Beloved" is such an important word – rich, resonant, pivotal – that I was delighted to find it in the readings for this week.

Lent begins with the cold smudge of ashes and ends in the stripped altars and desolation of Good Friday. Traditionally it's the season of penance and deprivation: a time of looking inwards and confronting the dark crevices and imperfections of the heart. For some this is a valuable exercise: bracing and creative. For others, it's dispiriting, crushing even, accentuating faults and weaknesses, inducing guilt and shame. Lent's ruthless self-examination can leave us feeling excluded, hopeless and anything but "beloved" of God.

I knew little about the keeping of "a good Lent" until I started going to a high Anglican church in central London in the late 1980s. Here, only yards from the bustle and sleaze of Oxford Street, the dramas of the Christian calendar are re-enacted with passion and precision, season by season. Leaving a few prejudices amidst the rubbish piled high on the pavement outside, I crossed the shrub-filled courtyard of All Saints and opened the door to find wisps of incense high in the rafters, and a few other surprises for someone with a Church of Scotland childhood.

One of the most unsettling of those surprises came one chill grey Spring day, when I went in to find all the crucifixes veiled in purple silk. I know now of course that this is common practice in many churches, but it was new to me then and I found the imagery troubling. The veiling made me feel brutally cut off from God, and from God's love for me in the cross. Perhaps I over-reacted; perhaps it was important to feel what I felt, however uncomfortable. But as I've relived the experience through subsequent Lents I've become more and more certain that Lent – with all its discipline and self-examination – can only be a time of real spiritual nourishment and growth if it is lived in the light of Easter, and in the confident knowledge that we are, each one of us, beloved of God.

Thought for the day
I too am the Beloved of God.

Prayer
Loving God, may our confidence in your love for us deepen, day by day.

Amen

Second Monday of Lent
Generosity

Dan 9:4-10; Ps 78; Lk 6:36-38

"Give, and there will be gifts for you: a full measure, pressed down, shaken together, and running over, will be poured into your lap."

(Luke 6:38)

In a windowless mud-brick store-room on the edge of the village, Tintadjabarte Walet Egafnalher pinches the hem of her robe taut, ready to catch her measure of grain in her lap. Her hair is woven with coins and cowrie shells, while silver anklets, heavy as shackles, glint at her feet. She carries no bag, but knotted into her skirts are tiny bundles of sugar and tea.

It's Lent 2000 and I am working in the small Tuareg (or Tamacheck as the people prefer to be known) settlement of Tintihigrene in Eastern Mali, making a programme for BBC World Service. Formerly nomads, the thirty or so families who live here were forced to abandon their centuries-old way of life when they lost everything in the great drought of 1984-85. I am wide-eyed at the biblical scenes and images played out in front of me: the sheep and goats, indistinguishable save for the droop of an ear or the curve of a snout; the rams caught in thorn bushes and the sore-footed camels; the goat-skin water bags slung over donkeys; the star-filled night skies and the shifting sand-tracks in the desert.

And here's another image: in the village cereal bank Tintadjabarte, a widow, receiving her full-measure of grain, over-flowing into her lap, so she can feed her family. It's provision more generous, and more secure, than she could have dreamed of in the old days of travelling for weeks in search of water in the desert, and she thanks God for his goodness and generosity.

An overflowing measure: the image is as exuberant as generosity itself, for generosity is dynamic and expansive, mirroring the very nature of God. Meanness, on the other hand, blocks and deadens.

But for generosity to be genuine it must be spontaneous, loving, free-spirited – as God's generosity is. Our reading of the words, "Give, and there will be gifts for you" needs to be careful, lest our generosity becomes self-seeking and manipulative. Julia Cameron, writing in *Heart Steps*, captures well the essence of generosity: "I am rooted in the wealth of God as a tree in rich soil. I share with others from God's unending abundance. As I share I am replenished. There is no lack, no shortfall, only flow."

No-one ever got poorer by being generous: as the destitute widow of 1 Kings discovered when she shared her last morsel with a stranger, the jar of meal was not spent, neither did the cruse of oil fail, according to the word of the Lord.

Thought for the day
We're each called to participate, with freedom and love, in the generous, life-giving flow of the Universe.

Prayer
Loving God, may your generous spirit flow in my veins.

Amen

Second Tuesday of Lent
Integrity

Is 1:10, 16-20; Ps 49; Mt 23:1-12

"They do not practise what they preach."

(Matthew 23:4)

"Come now, let us talk this over," says Yahweh.

(Isaiah 10:18)

Jesus had a thing about hypocrisy: a sensitivity, an alertness, an aversion. "They do not practise what they preach." Whenever he encountered hypocrisy, he exposed it. Sometimes this was done gently, in private; but when the hypocrites were harming others, the exposure was brutal and public.

I doubt if I'm alone in feeling a kind of vicarious guilt whenever I hear the words: "They do not practise what they preach." It's the same when I catch sight of a distant blue light flashing in my rear-view mirror. The words may not be addressed to me at that moment, but somehow, somewhere, I know they apply.

Hypocrisy, according to the dictionary, is split behaviour: the practice of professing standards and beliefs contrary to one's real character or actual behaviour, and especially the pretence of virtue or piety. It is at odds with the integrity to which I aspire, and to which we are called: the consistent adherence to moral principles; the qualities of honesty and wholeness.

It has always been easier for us to spot inconsistency and hypocrisy in others than in ourselves: Jesus' complaint about motes and beams makes that clear. But now modern psychology helps to explain why this is so. As our understanding of the shadow side of our nature grows, so our understanding of the "splitness" and inner conflict to which we are all prone is extended.

In his book *How to Befriend Your Shadow: Welcoming Your Unloved Side*, John Monbourquette writes: "The image evoked by the term 'Shadow', as first used by Jung ... represents well all the repressed material of the unconscious organised into a counterpart of what the conscious ego lives ... Like a light, the conscious self produces an unconscious dark area: the shadow." Which is why, sooner or later, and no matter how devout, we hear ourselves preaching what we do not practise.

Jesus condemns hypocritical behaviour and yet meets us with great kindness and compassion as we struggle with the conflict between what we know to be right and what we actually do. In the depths of that struggle it's easy to leave God out: to feel that we've got to get ourselves right before we can approach God. But God says, as he did to Isaiah, "Come now, let us talk this over." God invites us to share our struggle with him as openly and honestly as we can, and Lent is a heaven-sent opportunity to do just that.

Thought for the day
God says: Come now, let us talk this over.

Prayer
Loving God, may your Holy Spirit breathe in me until my thoughts are your thoughts.

Amen

Second Wednesday of Lent
Prosperity
Jer 18:18-20; Ps 30; Mt 20:17-28

"In my prosperity, I used to say: 'Nothing can ever shake me'. "

(Psalm 30:6)

Prosperity is relative: a Porsche perhaps, to a City broker; a cotton headscarf and an extra bar of soap to the wife of a Kenyan farmer.

Just how relative is highlighted in a wonderful book called *Material World: a Global Family Portrait*, written by Peter Menzel, and dedicated to the United Nations' International Year of the Family in 1994. The idea is simple, but the results profound.

It's a book of photographs of thirty families, from thirty countries, shown outside their homes with all their possessions. The families were chosen because they represented the average family in each country: average income, house, family size, occupation and religion. From Cuba to Uzbekistan, from Mali to the United States, from India to Albania: and although each family in the book would be prosperous in comparison with the poorest in their countries, the differences and inequalities, from country to country, make for dramatic and challenging page-turning.

Theologically speaking, prosperity is a difficult concept. Is it a sign of blessing: a manifestation of God's abundance and generosity? Is it a reward for being faithful and good? Or is it inevitably tainted by greed, injustice and exploitation? The questions give rise to heated and often self-justifying debate, and each position finds some support in a selective reading of scripture. But the Psalmist makes a vital contribution to that debate when he declares: "In my prosperity, I used to say: 'Nothing can ever shake me'. "

He points to the fact that prosperity isn't necessarily evil, but it is dangerous. It's dangerous because it masks our vulnerability, and it's out of our vulnerability that we relate most profoundly to God. The danger is that the more materially secure we are, the less aware we become of our day-by-day dependence on God. The self- confidence, complacency even, which goes so easily with the status and comfort of prosperity, can leak into our spiritual lives to sad and damaging effect.

I enjoyed the freedom and independence of working as a freelance enormously, but with that freedom comes a degree of insecurity. When contracts are coming to an end I can't help setting up a shining great golden calf called Security. It's a very powerful urge, but one I try to resist because I know that it's often at times of insecurity when I'm most immediately in touch with God, and when I'm most aware of the precision of his timing and the perfection of his provision.

Thought for the day

"*Material World* puts a human face on the issues of population, environment, social justice, and consumption and brilliantly illuminates the crucial question facing our species today: Can all five billion of us have all the things we want?" (from the fly-leaf of *Material World*)

Prayer

Loving God, have compassion on my fears and challenge my complacency. May I find my prosperity in knowing you.

Amen

Second Thursday of Lent

Pity me ...

Jer 17:5-10; Ps 1; Lk 16:19-31

"Father Abraham, pity me and send Lazarus to dip the tip of his finger in water and cool my tongue for I am in agony in these flames."

(Luke 16: 24)

At a complicated intersection beneath one of Delhi's low-slung concrete fly-overs I sit in my fume-filled black and yellow taxi, willing the lights to change. I clink a handful of five rupee coins in my palm and watch, out of the corner of my eye, the beggar's progress across the lanes of impatient traffic. He stands silently at the window of a silver Mercedes, his one misshapen, ulcerated leg swathed in grubby bandages. Steadying himself on a wooden crutch, he raises a cloven stump of an arm in salutation to the driver, and receives a single coin. I look at the lights again. Still red. My turn.

He taps on the window and I crank it down, just enough to reach through and give him the coins. I barely look at him. I want him not to be there. Not because I grudge a few rupees but because I am uncomfortable. I am ashamed. I think – as I always do in these situations – of Lazarus, and of the condemnation of the Rich Man. The sight of the beggar, and my paltry response to his need, unleashes complex and unsettling emotions: pity, impotence, guilt.

I'm intrigued by people who say they could never go to India because they couldn't bear the poverty, as if they were somehow ultra-sensitive souls – do they think the poverty is any less real because they don't see it? In a memorable opening to his book *No Full Stops in India*, Mark Tully writes: "How do you cope with the poverty? That must be the question I have been asked most frequently by visitors to India. I often reply, "I don't have to. The poor do." '

Tully continues: "The crocodile tears which have been shed for India's poor would flood the Ganges .... The fact that we, the fortunate of the world, still live with India's poverty is a scandal."

When Lazarus asked for pity, he needed not just an emotional response, but action.

Thought for the day
Our pity requires action to make it meaningful.

Prayer
Loving God, give me a heart full of pity, as your heart is, and a willingness to act on that pity, in your strength and in your name.

Amen

Second Friday of Lent
An empty well

Gen 37:3-4, 12-13, 17-28; Ps 104; Mt 21:33-43, 45-46

"... an empty well, with no water in it."

(Genesis 37:24)

Three hours south of Delhi by air-conditioned train and tourist department bus is the fabled ghost town of Fatehpur Sikri. A city of exquisite beauty, it was for 14 brief years, until 1585, the capital of the Mughal Empire. Built by the famed Emperor Akbar, the graceful pink-sandstone palaces and marble courtyards are, as *The Rough Guide to India* says, "an appropriate symbol of imperial power, and a sympathetic backdrop for the philosophical and artistic pursuits that were his passion." Fatehpur Sikri speaks not just of great power and wealth, but of taste and learning and art: the magnificent flowering of a civilisation.

But scarcely had it flowered, when it died. The river on which the city depended for its water supply changed its course, and the wells ran dry. The Emperor moved his court and within 20 years Fatehpur Sikri was deserted, symbolising something very different: not power and achievement, but human frailty and dependence.

In another of today's readings, Psalm 104, there are some breathless lines about water and our dependence on it. Addressing Yahweh, the Psalmist cries: "At your reproof the waters took flight, they fled at the sound of your thunder, cascading over the mountains, into the valleys .... You set springs gushing in ravines, running down between the mountains, supplying water for wild animals ... from your palace you water the uplands until the ground has had all that your heavens have to offer."

Without water we die. Even in the prosperous, profligate, industrialised world the image of an empty well retains its haunting potency, and how much more so in the south: in villages like Kiri, in central Mali. There, on the Koro plains, the soil is relatively rich, but the water table is desperately low and the local Dogon people have to dig wells by hand, through 80 metres of hard rock, before they reach water. Once the well is dug, the women spend hours each day in the hard labour of hauling water: "When you shake hands with a woman," says Hawa Dama, as we are introduced after a village meeting, "it's like touching wood".

A woman at a well: it's another of those biblical images that come dramatically to life for a twenty-first century visitor to the villages of rural Africa and India. It's an image which still combines physical reality and spiritual truth.

Thought for the day

"Whoever drinks this water will get thirsty again; but anyone who drinks the water that I shall give will never be thirsty again; the water that I shall give will turn into a spring inside him, welling up to eternal life." (John 4:13-14)

Prayer

Loving God, may we value water more as source and symbol: source of our physical life, symbol of our spiritual life, both sustained by you.

Amen

Second Saturday of Lent
What return can I make??

Jer 1:4-9; Ps 116; Lk 10:1-12, 17-20

"What return can I make to Yahweh for all his goodness to me?"

(Psalm 116:12)

In my experience eight-day Ignatian retreats usually consist of six days of agony and two days of resolution, or as St Ignatius would call it: "consolation". Occasionally the resolution comes sooner; once, it never came at all. But when it does come, that resolution is sweet indeed: it may be ecstatic or serene; a new insight or a longed-for answer; an almost subliminal shift or a dramatic transformation.

Towards the end of his Spiritual Exercises St Ignatius gives a gentle warning. Writing of the delight and peace of spiritual consolation and of the deep intimacy with God that retreatants can experience he advises them against making hasty commitments or major decisions while in the full flush of spiritual ecstasy. Instead, he urges retreatants to be cautious and discerning as they consider the wise response to their experience of God's goodness. Yet while he counsels caution and discernment, Ignatius knows that we do need to respond to God's goodness, and to ask, with the Psalmist: "What return can I make?"

As if answering his own question just a few lines later, the Psalmist says three things: "I will offer you thanksgiving ... I will walk in Yahweh's presence ... I will pay what I vowed." In other words, the best return I can make to God for his goodness to me is my Gratitude, my Presence, and my Action – in that order.

When we ask "What return can I make to God for all his goodness to me?" we're not asking "How can I pay God back for all he has done for me?" but rather, "What can I do to show God how much I love him?" Both the Psalmist and St Ignatius knew that we can never pay God back, and that's not what God wants. God wants us to love him, not be beholden to him.

When M Scott Peck finished the first draft of his worldwide best-seller *The Road Less Travelled* he went on retreat, and began to discover some of the riches of the monastic tradition. He writes: "Blindly, then, I stumbled (or stumbling, I was led) into a fresh but ancient world of daily offices ... of new twists to old words – contemplative, community, vocation – of feast days and spiritual directors; a world where solitude was respected and silence regarded as something to be sought after rather than avoided." Later, he was to collaborate on a book with a Carmelite nun, Sister (Sr) Marilyn Von Waldner. It's no surprise that their book begins with Thanksgiving: a hymn by Sr Marilyn called "The Lord has Done Great Things for Us", with the refrain: "And all that we did was in rejoicing, And all we could do was sing of the Lord."

Thought for the day

When I ask "What return can I make to God for all his goodness to me?" I am not asking "How can I pay God back for all he has done for me?" but rather "What can I do to show God how much I love him?"

Prayer

Loving God, show me how to show I love you.

Amen

Joseph Donders

Third week of Lent

Third Sunday of Lent

Breaking down and building up

Ex 20:1-17; Ps 19:8-10; 1 Cor 1:22-25; Jn 2:13-25

"Take all this out of here and stop using my Father's place as a market."

(John 2:16)

Visiting the temple, Jesus became angry. Furious. It was a rage that was so emotional and so striking that all four gospels tell us about it. There seems to be nothing left of the "sweet Jesus" we see in so many holy pictures and statues.

When he sees cattle dealers selling their animals and bankers changing money in the temple precincts he loses his temper. He even becomes violent. John notes that he made a whip out of cords and drove them out, all of them. It is as if he lost himself for a moment.

It is interesting to read that Jesus expresses his anger especially to the dove sellers. It is to them that he shouts: "Take all this out of here and stop using my Father's house as a market." Had his mother told him how at his circumcision she and Joseph had only been able to afford the sacrifice of some doves, and how they had been overcharged?

We are not the first among his disciples to be surprised by his anger and his violent outburst. So were his apostles. Trying to understand him they remembered some of the words of a psalm: "I am eaten up with zeal for your house" (Psalm 69). In that psalm the psalmist is not thinking of the building in Jerusalem as God's house. He is thinking of God's people. He is thinking of God's family. He is thinking of those who are the temple of God. The psalm continues to explain how his zeal made the psalmist a hated alien, a stranger to his own people, how he got mocked, despised and, finally, done away with. This quote from psalm 69 is a first hint in John's gospel of why Jesus is going to end up on the cross.

Why was Jesus so angry? The answer is simple and unforgettable. It was because he saw the exploitation of God's people by those who make money, business and greed the decisive factors in a world full of their victims.

Thought for the day
When you make a decision, what is the more significant influence: the Spirit of God, or the state of your bank account?

Let us pray
Almighty God, your Son, Jesus Christ, my Lord and my brother,
you challenge us to undo a system where money and profit prevail over solidarity with our sisters and brothers,
help me to live the life he lived among us, sharing his Spirit.

Amen

Third Monday of Lent
Healing

2 Kgs 5:1-15; Ps 41:2-3; 42:3-4; Lk 4:24-30

"... there were many lepers in Israel, but none of these was cured, except the Syrian, Naaman"

(Luke 4:27)

When Jesus returned to Nazareth for a weekend he was initially received very well. They had heard so many stories about his healing in Capernaum – his chasing away of evil, maybe even about his wine miracle in Cana – that his old neighbours were eager to see him. It was time for him to come home to be with them, his own kinfolk and acquaintances.

The synagogue in Nazareth was chock-a-block that Friday evening. They were all looking forward to hearing him, and maybe to witnessing some of his miracles. He did not disappoint them. He read a wonderful text to them from the prophet Isaiah. The Messianic prophecies would come to their fulfilment. The period of grace, the new age of the Jubilee, had started. It was all going to be great for them! It was good to belong to his circle, to the people he knew, to be his co-patriot.

Suddenly, all that changed. He began to speak about people who did not belong to their circle at all. He reminded them that Yahweh had reached out to a pagan widow at Zarephath, providing her with food through the prophet Elisha. He reminded them of how Yahweh had healed the Syrian officer, Naaman, through the intervention of the same prophet.

It was this wider care, beyond their neighbourhood, that they did not understand. Yahweh should only be for them. Jesus, too, should be for them – not for foreigners, or aliens, none of that nonsense. They got so upset about his challenge to share God's gifts with those others, that they sprang to their feet, hustled him out of the synagogue, wanting to kill him.

They manifested a dynamics that is still rampant in our world. God bless my country! Yet, the healing that Jesus came to bring to this world, and that we his disciples stand for, is for all. It is a global one.

Thought for the day

"My welfare is only possible if I acknowledge my unity with all the people of the world". (Leo Tolstoy, 1828-1910)

Let us pray

Loving and eternal God, help me to overcome the difficulty in believing that you love others in the same way I experience that you love me. That you gave them life just as you gave life to me, to share in yours.

Amen

Third Tuesday of Lent

Paying our debt

Dn 3:25, 34-43; Ps 24; Mt 18:21-35

"... Were you not bound, then, to have pity on your fellow-servant, just as I had pity on you?"

(Matthew 18:33)

Matthew's "Good News Report" is a community gospel. He uses Jesus' words to develop a community sense. A community in which Jesus is our universal brother.

Communities have their difficulties. So has our global community. We can philosophise, write and speak in glowing terms about all kinds of so-called "spiritual" issues but there are also hard facts we have to take into account if we want to be realistic. Jean-Paul Sartre, the French existentialist philosopher, once pointed out that any theory that does not take into account the scarcity of goods in our world is of no use.

In Matthew's gospel those hard facts are not overlooked by Jesus. Jesus does not offer pious platitudes. His words "cut more incisively than any two-edged sword... [passing] judgment on secret emotions and thoughts" (Hebrews 4:12).

One of the issues that causes difficulties in any community is that of the debts community members might have among themselves. In Matthew's gospel Jesus' ideas on lending and borrowing are clear. In the first place, if anyone needs to borrow money and you would be able to lend it to him, Jesus' principle is: "Give to the one who asks of you, and do not turn your back on one who wants to borrow" (Matthew 5:42).

Jesus' parable of today tells us what we must do next. When the master in the story hears that a servant, whose debt of ten thousand talents he had forgiven, refused to cancel the debt of a colleague of a hundred denarii, and even had his debtor arrested, he says: "Were you not bound, then, to have pity on your fellow-servant, just as I had pity on you?"(Matthew 18:33). No wonder that Christian organisations such as CAFOD take a lead in campaigns to cancel the repayments of international debts that rich countries are still demanding from poor countries.

Thought for the day

It is better to give than to lend.

Let us pray

Almighty and eternal God,
let me not get lost in a love for you that would forget about the needs of the others around me.
Help me to understand that their needs and worries are the needs and worries of my own heart.
I ask you this through Christ, our compassionate Brother.

Amen

Third Wednesday of Lent
On not forgetting

Dt 4:1, 5-9; Ps 147; Mt 5:17-19

"Do not forget the things which you yourselves have seen, or let them slip from your heart as long as you live."

(Deuteronomy 4:9)

It was Moses who told his people never to forget the misery they had experienced in Egypt and never to forget how Yahweh had rescued them from that misery. He told them to tell their children and their children's children. The memory of those events should remain alive in their hearts and minds. Its remembrance should serve as a guiding star during their lives. Elie Wiesel, a Jewish concentration camp survivor wrote, "We have to remember that we can't remember .... Memory must not stop." The memory of past horrors can help to prevent them happening again.

In today's gospel Jesus, too, warns us not to forget, just as he did not forget. He did not come to eradicate or abolish anything. He told us that the old should be faithfully remembered, while living and building up the new. It is a lesson all of us can apply to ourselves. We should not forget. The older ones among us might remember the horrors they went through during war time or other times of crisis.

All of us are confronted every day with the horrors of our time, even if they do not affect us immediately. News broadcasts, daily papers, and internet messages bombard us daily with images and stories illustrating injustice and misery throughout the world.

That is not all that there is to be seen. All over the world people of good will are coming together in organisations, parishes and communities to offset these horrors. Helping where help is needed and assisting in the reconstruction and development of societies, in such a way that one day no outside help will be needed any more. Those memories should not be forgotten either. The Spirit of Jesus is at work through us. Even one good memory might be our salvation today. The victory will be ours! The guarantee of that victory is given to us by the event we celebrate at Easter, Jesus' Resurrection.

Thought for the day

"It is a poor sort of memory that only works backwards." (Lewis Carroll, 1832-1898)

Let us pray

Loving God, I am so grateful that you sent Jesus Christ among us, who walked with us, faced the evil in his world and overcame it for all of us. Help me to follow his example, living with his Spirit in my world.

Amen

Third Thursday of Lent
The way ahead
Jr 7:23-28; Ps 94; Lk 11:14-23

"Anyone who does not gather in with me throws away."
(Luke 11:23)

In his 1990 encyclical on mission Pope John Paul II used as his first quote from the Bible Paul's letter to the Corinthians, "Woe to me if I do not preach the Gospel!" (1 Corinthians 9:16). This quote is immediately followed by a second one from John's Gospel: "May all be one ... so that the world may believe that it was you who sent me" (John 17:21).

The two sayings relate to each other. If the oneness Jesus prayed for is not going to be realized, the world and its humanity are really doomed. It will be one world or no world.

Jesus was so convinced of the need for this oneness that he was willing to give his life "to gather into one the scattered children of God" (John 11:52). In other words, he gave his life to realize that oneness.

The gospels frequently mention this "gathering" mission of Jesus. Jesus himself does it every time he calls himself a shepherd who is bringing together his flock. One afternoon he is sitting on a hillside overlooking Jerusalem and he sighs saying: "Jerusalem, Jerusalem, you who kill the prophets and stone those sent to you, how many times I yearned to gather your children together as a hen gathers her brood under her wings, but you were unwilling!" (Luke 13:34).

In her book *The Way Ahead* Soozi Holbeche has a story about the connection between humanity and the repair needed by the world. This repair or mending of the world is known in Hebrew as "tikkun olam". The story is about a teacher who tore up a map of the world in small pieces, and thinking it an impossible task, gave it to a recalcitrant student to put it together again. Within ten minutes the boy is back, the task completed. Astounded, the teacher asked him how he did it. The boy replied: "When I turned the pieces over, I found a torn-up man. I put him together, and when I looked at the other side the world was whole again."

Thought for the day

"I look upon the whole world as my fatherland, and every war has to me the horror of a family feud." (Helen Keller, 1880-1968).

Let us pray

Jesus, help me not only to pray with you, as you asked us to do, teaching us the "Our Father", help me also to live for the hearing of that prayer all through my life, in each and every decision.

Amen.

Third Friday in Lent
Are you listening?
Hos 14:2-10; Ps 80; Mk 12:28-34

"This is the first: listen...!"

(Mark 12:29)

We all think we know the answer Jesus gave when one of the scribes asked him about the most important commandment. But do we really know how Jesus answered the question? Before he says, "loving God with all our heart, with all your soul, with all your mind and with all your strength ... [and] you must love your neighbour as yourself," he asks us to do something else: "This is the first, listen, Israel!" (Mark 12:29-30).

Listening is the beginning of it all. This is even physically true. The first sense we develop while still in our mother's womb is that of listening to the many sounds around us and the last faculty that closes down when we die is often our ability to hear.

We are not going to do anything about the world or its people if we are not willing to listen. We need to listen to the voices of those around us. We need to listen to the stories of the people throughout our global village. The psychologist and spiritual author Jean Houston tells us that we need to develop the "habit of multicultural deep listening." This is the kind of listening she thinks is critical to the survival of our world and its population.

You can also say it in a different way. In a well known contemporary hymn we remind ourselves that "God listens to the cries of the poor". Being equipped with God's Spirit we ourselves should do the same. Even if we have already decided that we are going to offer our help to people, first we must listen to them. We can only help them, and ourselves, through a love that listens. Saint Benedict, the founder of the Benedictines, wrote: "Listen, my children, with the ear of your heart."

This does not mean that we should only listen to the cries for help and mercy around us. We should also listen to the joy and fulfilment around us: the noise a child makes when happily jumping around, a cat that purrs, a conversation that brightens our day, the hubbub of a family meal, and music that makes us dance. There are many voices that want to be heard, from outside and from inside of us – even the voice of God.

Thought for the day

"The only way to love a person is not, as the stereotyped Christian notion is, to coddle them and bring them soup when they are sick, but by listening to them ... " (Brenda Ueland, 1892-1985).

Let us pray

Almighty and loving God, listen to my prayer.
Teach me to listen to your voices that come to me in the joys and the sorrows surrounding me. Help me to become an active listener.
Take away my deafness, open my closed ears,
and let me listen just like you listened to us when you sent your Son Jesus.

Amen

Third Saturday of Lent
Faithfulness

Hos 5:15-6: 6; Ps 50; Lk 18:9-14

"For faithful love pleases me, not sacrifice."

(Hosea 6:5)

Hosea is a prophet who wants to call his people back to God. He pleads: "Come let us return to Yahweh!" (Hosea 6:1). It is striking how the prophet stresses a return to a faithful love rather than merely to attendance at the temple. In the temple one busies oneself with all kinds of ritual sacrifices, often forgetting that one's relation to God should lead to further consequences outside of the temple.

It is a demand we might apply in our own lives. What about our liturgical celebrations with their complex rites and rituals? What about our church buildings, the decorations, the garments, the choirs, the incense and the music? The famous Swiss theologian Hans Urs von Balthasar once remarked that the nicer the tabernacle, the heavier its doors, the more expensive its decorations, the better Jesus is isolated from one's daily life.

Why do we go to church services? How different are we when we have returned home? Do we call ourselves followers of Jesus Christ simply because of our faithfulness to the ritual? What happened to God's word? How do we respond to God's word? What is its influence on our lives once we have left the church building?

In today's gospel Jesus speaks about a person caught up in the temple's ritual. He is a Pharisee, who in his prayer in the temple tells God how faithful he is to all its formalities. But Jesus says that he leaves the temple without being justified. Jesus then compares his attitude with that of the tax collector, a man who asks for forgiveness, knowing perfectly well that neither he, nor the world in which he lives, are as they should be. He is aware of his carelessness, his dishonesty, his ignorance, his frailty and his need to change himself and the world in which he lives.

God asks for faithful love. A love that is going to change the face of the earth in its faithfulness to God's Spirit. "For faithful love pleases me, not sacrifice, knowledge of God, not burnt offerings" (Hosea 6:6).

Thought for the day

"Religion without humanity is a poor human stuff." (Sojourner Truth, 1797-1883)

Let us pray

Dear Jesus, who in your love for us came among us to restore the unity of our human family, help me to share in your love for all of us, breaking your bread and sharing your wine, realizing the one body we are.

Amen

Joan Chittister

Fourth week of Lent

Fourth Sunday of Lent

God's messengers

2 Chr 36:14-16; Ps 136; Eph 2:4-10; Jn 3:14-21

"Yahweh continuously sent them word through his messengers ... but they ridiculed the messengers of God."

(2 Chronicles 36:15-16)

It is so easy to think that scripture, as we know it, is a kind of dead letter event, a celebration of history not of life, a nostalgia piece about another people – more wicked than we, more hard-hearted than we, more careless of God than we. Certainly less "religious" than we are. After all, we know ourselves to be good: we keep the feasts – Lent, for instance. But the Hebrews kept their feasts, too. We tithe and contribute and throw a penny or two into a poor man's pocket on the way to our cars. Sometimes we even make substantial donations to good things. But the Hebrews honored the gleaning laws that promised the leftovers of the harvest to the poor, as well. And like the Hebrews to whom God sent prophet after prophet, we get messengers aplenty from God to recall us, too, from our sinful ways.

Scientists are messengers. They tell us that we are burning out the ozone layer, drying up farmlands and melting the polar ice cap. But we resist air pollution laws on the grounds that it will cut industrial profits.

Economists are messengers. They tell us that we are using slave labour – child labour to make the designer shoes and suits and computer parts we want. But we tell ourselves that six cents an hour for a fourteen hour day is all an Indian child needs.

Ethnologists are messengers. They tell us that the borders of the world are seeping, cultures are merging. The poor are getting poorer everyday, even in the richest nations in the world. But the privileged carry on certain of their entitlement, both personal and political, to resources and power.

And the scriptures, the gospel, are messengers to us. Today the Book of Chronicles reminds us that "they kept mocking the messengers of God ... until there was no remedy." The scriptures are clear: Today's readings are not about another people in another world. This time it is we who must sit up and listen to the messengers God is sending us.

Thought for the day

Let those with ears to hear, hear what the Spirit is saying to the churches.

Prayer

God of mercy, give us ears to hear what you call us to repent in our own time.

Amen

Fourth Monday of Lent
A confusing answer
Is 65:17-21; Ps 26:2, 4-6, 11-13; Jn 4:43-54

"'Go home,' said Jesus, 'Your son will live.'"

(John 4:50)

God sent the prophets to remind us of who we are and what we are to be doing with our lives. "And what does the Lord require of you?" Scripture asks. The answer is a stark one: "To act justly and to love mercy and to walk humbly with your God." What?!

The answer confuses us. It takes our puny little religious concepts, the ones we attribute to God in order to make ourselves feel good, and turns them upside down. A people given to religious bartering – so many turtle doves, so many bullocks, so much lenten fasting done to keep God happy with us – is told that sacrifice is not the answer. Only conversion of life really counts where the God of gods is concerned. In fact, it is the ultimate sacrifice asked for here, this putting down of the greed we call "progress" and the vindictiveness we call "justice" and the pride we call "success."

Jesus is what the prophets had in mind as the one who pleased God, as the one who is the sign of God, as the one we are to follow. But that's where Lent gets real.

It is the justice of the Jesus who cured Romans as well as Jews that we are expected to practice in a world full of starving foreigners and political enemies and children without health insurance. It is the mercy of the Jesus who lifted up the woman taken in adultery and befriended the tax collector in the tree that we are expected to bring to the world around us.

It is simplicity of the Jesus who "became just like us" and did not consider "being equal to God a thing to be clung to" that we are to show to those on the social ladder beneath us – that is the real Lenten fasting God desires of us. Lent leads us to ask ourselves how much of any of this kind of sacrifice we are really doing. Justice, mercy and simplicity of life – the marks of the Jesus we follow to Calvary – are the only things that really make Lent, Lent.

Thought for the day
It's easy to pretend to be religious but being it .... Ah, there is the part that makes a real difference.

Prayer
Loving God, fire in us a desire to be the justice, the mercy and the humility of Jesus for which all our fasts and sacrifices prepare us.

Amen

Fourth Tuesday of Lent
The irrepressible troublemaker

Ezek 47:1-9, 12; Ps 45:2-3, 5-6, 8-9; Jn 5:1-3, 5-16

"There is a pool called Bethesda .... One man there had an illness that had lasted thirty-eight years."

(John 5:2, 5)

Jesus is causing trouble again. The one for whom the world waited to fulfill the prophet's message of justice, mercy and simplicity is healing an invalid. On the Sabbath.

In today's gospel reading, Jesus departs again from the old ways to show a new way, a way in which the person is more important than any law, however revered, which denies a person life. Such reordering of priorities in a very orderly system does not, however, make a person popular with the system. This Jesus is an irrepressible troublemaker for system types. And he does it over and over again. He brings scroungy-looking women into rich men's houses. He eats and drinks with low life. He challenges the pious on the validity of their piety. And then he violates the greatest law of all, the sanctity of the Sabbath. On the Sabbath, everything stops: working stops, cooking stops, selling stops. Even curing cripples is not excuse enough for a person to break the Sabbath. But he does.

The idea is cataclysmic. The situation itself is even worse. On the Sabbath Jesus heals a man who has been crippled for thirty-eight years. Why the rush? Why not simply wait and do the thing another day? That way you satisfy both the system and the situation. But no, there is an even more important message here.

A crippled man has been sitting on the edge of a healing pool for thirty-eight years. Why? The scripture is clear: "Because there is no one," he says, "to carry me down." It's a stunning message: all the Lenten fasts in the world, all the rigorous religious practices on the planet, will not substitute for our carrying the crippled of the world down to the pools that will heal them. We must carry the hungry to food, and the homeless to shelter, and the beaten to hospitals and the children to safety and the innocent civilians of political wars to the things that make for peace. And especially on God's day.

Lent is a shocking time. It reveals the irreligion of our religion. It reveals us to ourselves.

Thought for the day
For those who like the security that keeping the law can bring, Jesus is a problem to be dealt with.

Prayer
Give us, O God, the courage to do what must be done
for the poor however many the laws that
seek to make that impossible.

Amen

Fourth Wednesday of Lent

The generosity of God

Is 49:8-15; Ps 144:8-9, 13-14, 17-18; Jn 5:17-30

"The Father loves the Son and shows him everything he himself does, and he will show him even greater things than these."

(John 5:20)

Today's gospel reading is a subtle and disarming one. It sounds very lofty when it is actually about something very simple. It seems to be only about Jesus but it is just as surely about us. We like to see it as some kind of proof passage for the divinity of Jesus. And surely it is. But it is far more than that, as well.

My mother ironed every Tuesday morning. She set up the board in the den and went through the large clothes basket one shirt, one dress, one pair of pants at a time. And I stood next to her the whole long day, over a tiny ironing board, doing my imaginary same. That's how I came to understand this gospel.

Jesus uses a very homely metaphor here for a very profound truth: children imitate their parents. Children watch what their parents do and they do the same. As the parents work, children follow them around in an attempt to do exactly what they do. And that's where the gospel becomes our gospel.

When we see what God has done in this world – created all colours and races of people and called all of them "good," provided a planet pregnant with life, lush with gifts, connected us to every species on earth for our well-being, spun us into orbit in a galaxy of glitter – and still "goes on working". The implications for us are awesome. Overwhelming. Morally demanding. Immense. We must do for others what God has done for us.

Clearly Lent is not the time to be dour. Lent is the time to contemplate, to "put on the mind of God," to recognise our place in this universe and to live our lives as God shows us: oozing generosity, intent on equality, just in all our ways, bringers of beauty, promoters of life and open to new possibilities always.

Then, like Jesus, we can claim to be one with the One who does indeed go on working. In us. What we do or don't do with this world will determine it. Now that is an awesome thought.

Thought for the day

To follow Jesus is to learn to think like him, to begin to see the world as God sees the world.

Religion to be true must be more about contemplation than it is about practices.

Prayer

Great God, enable us to "put on the mind of Christ" and so come to see the whole world differently.

Amen

Fourth Thursday of Lent
God's trap
Ex 32:7-14; Ps 105:19-23; Jn 5:31-47

"God then relented over the disaster which he had intended to inflict on his people."

(Exodus 32:14)

Trapped. God is trapped. The Israelites, worried by the fact that Moses is late coming down from Mount Sinai, have abandoned Yahweh and gone running back to the gods of the tribe. God wants to wipe them out and start over again with people who are faithful, who cooperate, who believe. But Moses, leader of this lost and frightened people, reasons with God. It is in God's self-interest, Moses argues, not to destroy the Israelites as they deserve. How could other people trust a God who did not keep promises? What would the world think if the people God saved from the Egyptians were destroyed by God instead?

It's a charming story. We're inclined to smile about it. But the fact is that it's true and no one knows that better than we.

Honour the Lord your God, God tells a people who have begun to worship false gods of greed and power, gobbling up the world and holding it hostage to unrestrained military might.

Keep Holy the Sabbath, God tells a people who take little or no time in life for contemplation of their own place in the universe.

Don't steal, God tells a people who daily take the resources of the poor for a pittance and a laugh. Don't lie, God tells a people who cheat the world on wages and welfare and political motives.

Don't wallow in sins of the flesh, God tells a people who lust after the servitude of all the women of the world.

Don't kill, God tells a people, for whom life from the womb to the tomb has become a disposable commodity.

Don't neglect the family, God tells a people for whom family has become more a biological trick than a life-long commitment. Don't set your eyes on getting someone else's property, God tells a people who teach one another to want everything they see.

Indeed, God is trapped by the God-ness of fidelity and mercy. And so you and I, too, are given day after day to put down our false gods and become what we are meant to be.

Thought for the day

Even in our weakness God stays close by, waiting for us to realise that the puny little gods on whom we have spent life – money, power, profit and satiety – do not satisfy.

Prayer

You are our life, O God. Give us the insight to see that your ways alone give life.

Amen

Fourth Friday of Lent
Keep on keeping on
Wis 2:1, 12-22; Ps 33:16, 18, 19-21; Jn 7: 1-2, 10, 25-30

"They wanted to arrest him then, but because his hour had not yet come no one laid a hand on him."

(John 7:30)

Scripture is full of stories about Jesus the wonder-worker. But it also full of stories about Jesus the man, the one who knows the price to be paid for justice.

Jesus has been calling the system for years now. He has exposed the inconsistencies in the Law. He has riddled the thinking of the Pharisees. He has broken the Sabbath for the sake of the poor. He has preached a gospel of mercy and justice, healing outcasts and castigating officials. He has practiced inclusion in a closed society. He has done everything the Word of God demands in a godless world. He has confronted both popular religion and dishonest politics. And, scripture says, Jesus knew that they "were looking for an opportunity to kill him."

What's worse, even the people who know him best call him crazy. Worse, Jesus knows it. He knows, too, that one way or another his days are numbered. But that's not really the point of this gospel. The point is that he goes on despite it all. And that may be the most important thing of all.

It is one thing to lose; it is entirely another to realise that you are losing but persist despite it.

We all stand to be intimidated. We all wonder sometime what's the use, why bother? We're getting nowhere. Nothing is changing. In fact, things are actually getting worse: Pollution rates are up. Poverty indices are up. Militarism is up. And people think we're crazy. So why go on?

The ancients tell the story of an old woman who ran through the streets shouting "Power, greed and corruption .... Power, greed and corruption." One day a child stopped her saying, "Old woman, no one is listening to you. Why do you keep on shouting?" And the old woman said, "Oh, my child, I don't shout in order to change them. I shout so that they can't change me." It's not what we do, it's what we are that counts.

Lent reminds us to go on calling for the justice of Jesus just when we most want to quit.

Thought for the day

The ancients say, "If you want to know if your work on earth is finished, if you're still alive, it isn't." Keep on keeping on.

Prayer

Your time is not our time, O God. Give us the strength to go on doing what we must even when it seems that we're not getting anywhere.

Amen

Fourth Saturday of Lent
Speaking out
Jer 11:18-20; Ps 7:2-3, 9-12; Jn 7:40-52

"The people could not agree about him."

(John 7:44)

Today's scriptures are about plotting and planning, conspiracy and condemnation. Jeremiah and Jesus are each on somebody's list for elimination. The Israelites want the prophet Jeremiah to stop reminding them about the Covenant – which they have no intention of hearing. The chief priests and Pharisees want Jesus to stop prophesying the imminent coming of the reign of God in him – which they argued was impossible because he did not fit their expectations of the messiah.

Those elements are obvious. What is not so obvious, but much more important for us in the long run, perhaps, is the fact that today's scriptures are also about more than what Jeremiah or Jesus do in each of them. They are also about what the people around them do not do in the face of all the plotting and the planning, the conspiracy and condemnations. And that's where you and I come in.

Nicodemus stands in for all of us here. Nicodemus is himself a Pharisee. He is respected in the city, a member of the inner circle of religious leaders, educated, privileged, secure. Nicodemus, remember, "had gone to Jesus at night." He had crept in to talk to Jesus when he would not be noticed, in other words, when his public reputation wouldn't be hurt by it, when he could talk to Jesus and pay no price for doing so. But now, when it counts, all that Nicodemus manages to do is to raise a feeble legal question about Jesus' right to defend himself.

He doesn't defend Jesus himself. He doesn't speak on his behalf. He doesn't witness to the holiness of his actions. He asks a timid question and when it is soundly rebutted, he says not another word.

Who doesn't know the cost of speaking out against the political or ecclesiastical dictums of the day, thought good by many but more than open to discussion if not debate in the light of the "whole law of God and the prophets."

The lenten question that confronts us all today is a sad but clear one: For whom do you and I speak when the social stakes are high? Or do we simply stay quiet in order to be accepted by those whose opposition will cost us: the politicians, the family, the pastor, the neighbours, the socialites, the boss, the movers and shakers in town?

But if that's the case, what's been the use of all the lenten prayers and fasting anyway?

Thought for the day

There is no such thing as powerlessness. There is only the decision to do what we can or not.

Prayer

Give us, O God, the courage to speak out even when everyone else is silent.

Amen

Michael Nuttall

Fifth week of Lent

Fifth Sunday of Lent

A dramatic meeting

Jer 31:31-34; Ps 51:3-4, 12-15; Heb 5:7-9; Jn 12:20-30

"Sir, we wish to see Jesus."

(John 12:21)

It was no easy or automatic thing for a group of Gentiles to have access to a Jewish rabbi. For Jews in the time of Jesus had no dealings with Gentiles any more than with Samaritans (see John 4:9). Even in modern times this can be a problem. I remember how, on a Christmas pastoral visit to Jerusalem with Archbishop Desmond Tutu in 1989, our presence at the Western Wall was resented by some ultra-orthodox Jews who expressed their antipathy to "goyim" being in the vicinity.

The Greeks who wanted to see Jesus were in Jerusalem to worship at the Passover festival. They would have heard that he had driven the traders and money-changers out of the court of the Gentiles in the temple and had spoken brave words: "Is it not written 'My house shall be called a house of prayer for all the nations'? But you have made it a den of robbers" (see Mark 11:17). Here was someone they would love to meet. They went about it diplomatically. Have a word, they thought to themselves, with the one called Philip, for he is from Bethsaida in Galilee where there are Gentiles. Philip hesitates; this is a big request for the Teacher. He goes to Andrew, who had earlier fetched Simon Peter his brother and brought him to Jesus (see John 1:41-42), and who had brought the young boy to Jesus with his few loaves and fish (see John 6:9). Andrew knows how to deal with these things. So Philip and Andrew go to Jesus together. "There are some Greeks who want to see you."

Jesus's response is amazing. It's not "Bring them in; let's have some tea", but "The hour has come for the Son of Man to be glorified" (verse 23). For him a fundamental purpose of the cross, which is coming his way, is to bring about a costly reconciliation between Jew and Gentile, slave and free, male and female, rich and poor, black and white, resident and alien. This will be the glory: to break down, once and for all, the dividing walls of hostility (see Ephesians 2:14), to build a new community.

This is our vocation also.

Thought for the Day

"Love for neighbour is a movement from hostility to hospitality." (Henri Nouwen)

Prayer

Grant us, gracious God, hearts and minds so hospitable to others that we shall reflect the mind of Christ in his Passion.

Amen

Fifth Monday of Lent
A brilliant intervention

Dn 13:1-9, 15-17, 19-30, 33-62; Ps 22 22; Jn 8:1-11

"Teacher, this woman has been caught in the act of adultery."

(John 8:4)

Jesus finds himself in a situation of considerable danger. He is up against the self-righteous religious establishment of his day and the sacrosanct teaching of Moses. Will he conform or will he go against the grain?

A woman is standing before him, caught (they said) in an act of adultery. The poignancy and embarrassment would not have escaped Jesus. Nor would the realisation that it takes two to commit an act of adultery. Why had only one of them been brought? Why only the woman?

Are these the reasons why Jesus bent down and wrote with his finger on the ground? Embarrassed, thoughtful, indignant? The need to "doodle" and not to be rushed into a hasty response? The scene is deeply evocative.

Then there comes his brilliant intervention. "Let him who is without sin among you be the first to throw a stone at her." Here is the answer to all sense of moral superiority and judgmentalism. It is akin to the statement: "There, but for the grace of God, go I." To their credit, the religious leaders all slunk away, one by guilty one. It is wise to acknowledge weakness and sinfulness in ourselves, to be careful about pointing a finger at another.

Jesus's twofold response to the woman was masterly. He did not condemn, nor did he condone. "Neither do I condemn you; go, and do not sin again." His affirmation and counsel were the opposite of the humiliating treatment given her by the religious leaders. Instead of harsh discrimination against her as adulterer and woman, she heard from Jesus words of respect and firmness in an attitude of mercy.

John's gospel gives a prominent place to the role of women and our Lord's affirmation of them. There is Mary his mother at the wedding in Cana (chapter 2), the Samaritan divorcee and evangelist (chapter 4), the Bethany sisters (chapters 11 and 12), the three Marys at the cross (chapter 19) and Mary Magdalene the first witness of the resurrection, first apostle of the resurrection to the others (chapter 20). All this is highly relevant in situations of gender discrimination today.

Thought for the Day

The pursuit of justice in society requires boldness and also prudence with sensitivity, a willingness to bend down and write with our finger on the ground.

Prayer

Righteous God, grant us courage, grant us wisdom for the living of these days.

Amen

Fifth Tuesday of Lent
Why pray?
Num 21:4-9; Ps 102:2-3, 16-18, 19-21; Jn 8:21- 30

"So Moses prayed for the people."

(Numbers 21:7)

Intercessory prayer – that is, prayer for others – is in some ways a mystery we shall never fully understand. Does God need our prayers in order to act? Surely not, but he may want them in order to engage us with his activity. God certainly does not need an information service, as though he becomes aware of situations of war or illness or whatever because we tell him about them. What about the outcome of our prayers? Why is it that some seem to have a fruition that is positive while others do not? For some people there may be a cloud with a silver lining, for others a cloud of unknowing.

One thing is sure: our intercessory prayer helps us to become more caring and sensitive in God's beloved world and therefore, knowingly or unknowingly, agents of his just and loving purposes. To intercede is to share in God's caring, to be transformed into a greater openness to the suffering of the world, to be goaded into action of some kind. It is to live representatively.

The enclosed Anglican religious community the Society of the Precious Blood has a house in the hills of Lesotho, and it was said that during the years of South Africa's struggle for political liberation the Sisters there fought apartheid on their knees. It could even be said that their hidden work of intercession was as important as the prophetic stand of a Desmond Tutu, a Beyers Naude and a Denis Hurley. Such is the case with all who are willing to travel the difficult journey – sometimes the dark night – of faithful prayer.

Moses, too, was a prophetic liberator of his people from political oppression in Egypt. "Let my people go," he demanded of Pharoah. He also prayed constantly for his people. The Book of Numbers says that he was very meek, more than anyone on the face of the earth (12:3). Because of that God would meet with him face to face and speak to him "as a man speaks to his friend" (Exodus 33:11). In Moses we have an authentic combination of prophet, pastor and pray-er.

Thought for the day
The world is in a fragile condition; handle it with prayer.

Prayer
The things, good Lord, that we pray for, give us the grace to labour for. (St Thomas More)

Fifth Wednesday of Lent
The appearance of the fourth

Dan 3:14-20, 91-92, 95; Ps Dan 3:52-56; Jn 8:31-42

"I see four men loose, walking in the midst of the fire, ... and the appearance of the fourth is like a son of the gods."

(Daniel 3:25)

When Desmond Tutu was campaigning for justice in the dark days of apartheid South Africa, the story of Daniel and his two friends unharmed in the burning fiery furnace was for him a constant source of inspiration and encouragement. "The appearance of the fourth" in the same fire is a reminder that the God with whom we have to do is indeed our Emmanuel, "God with us". It is not easy to see this when evil appears to have the upper hand. Archbishop Tutu wrote that at times, to keep one's morale up, it was necessary to whistle in the dark, and pray: "God, we know that you are in control, but can you not make it a little more obvious?"

In the midst of human suffering or the struggle for a just social order, we can sometimes miss or forget the vital importance of the fourth dimension – that is, "the appearance of the fourth" with us in it all. There is a temptation to try to manage on our own, whereupon our concerns begin to lose their cutting edge. In South Africa we found that the nourishment to be derived from prayer and worship was essential for the pursuit of justice in society. Desmond Tutu was first and foremost a person of prayer and meditation, wedded to the daily Eucharist and the daily

Office. He would insist on taking his brother bishops regularly into retreat together. From that environment of waiting upon God he would receive what he called 'divine nudges' to hold a protest march, visit a township in turmoil, or beard a state president or some other politician in his den. The Christian championship of justice needs to be rooted in what King Nebuchadnezzar found: the participation of a fourth, 'like a son of the gods', the divine presence with us in the fiery furnaces we confront.

According to Michael Ramsey, who was Archbishop of Canterbury in the 1960s, "a saint is one who has a strange nearness to God and makes God real and near to other people ....He shares and bears the griefs of his fellows, and he feels the world's pain with a heightened sensitivity; but with that sensitivity he has an inner serenity of an unearthly kind which brings peace and healing to other people." (Margaret Duggan, ed. *Through the Year with Michael Ramsey*, pages 38-39).

Thought for the day

He (God) said not
Thou shalt not be travailed
Thou shalt not be tempested
Thou shalt not be afflicted
But he said
Thou shalt not be overcome.   (Julian of Norwich)

Prayer

Christ of the Passion, be our companion in our fiery ordeals, whether personal or on the larger canvas of a national or international challenge.

Amen

Fifth Thursday in Lent
Renewing the earth
Gn 17:3-9; Ps 104; Jn 8:51-59

"You set the earth on its foundations, so that it should never be moved."

(Psalm 104:5)

At the heart of the Church's quest for a just order in society – whether in politics or economics, in sexuality or whatever – lies the creation narrative in the opening chapter of the Bible (Genesis 1) where humankind, both male and female, is made in the image and likeness of God. This teaching makes any injustice not only ethically wrong, but also a blasphemy.

The image of God principle can be taken further. It is set within the whole created order, which in every part, great and small, reflects the divine handiwork. "When you send forth your Spirit they are created; you renew the face of the earth"(Psalm 104:30).

Most of our concerns, wherever we live, tend understandably to be people-centred, but we dare not ignore the issue of what we are doing to our natural environment, which often amounts to nothing less than the rape of our fragile planet through pollution and exploitation. Adrian Hastings, writing in *The Tablet* in the millennium year 2000, said graphically and alarmingly: "Babies born at the start of the new millennium will be faced in their sixties, if not before, with a crisis in human history so unprecedented that it is hard to imagine it ....The most uncontollable factor will be global warming." Mount Everest provides an ominous illustration. The glacier from which Hillary and Tenzing began their ascent fifty years ago has been melting and has retreated about three miles since that time. Other icefields in the area are also shrinking. More to the point, it is predicted that, if the present trend continues, low-lying countries like Bangladesh and the Netherlands will eventually be completely covered by the rising waters.

There are dissenting voices on the subject of global warming, and no doubt the subject needs further rigorous thought and debate. The fact of undue exploitaion and pollution is not in doubt, and what is needed, as with a human scourge like Aids, is a willingness on every side, individual and corporate, to take responsibility and put specific policies in place to reverse the trend. The Church also needs to be part of this process and to give a prophetic lead.

Thought for the Day
"The earth is the Lord's and the fullness thereof." (Psalm 24:1)

Prayer
Help us, creator God, to remember that the earth does not belong to us, but that we belong to it and to you. Make us good stewards of your handiwork.

Amen

Fifth Friday of Lent
The true prophet
Jr 20:10-13; Ps 17; Jn 10:31-42

"I hear many whispering. Terror is on every side!"

(Jeremiah 20:10)

It is not easy to be the Lord's prophet, to throw down the gauntlet at the perpetrators of injustice and say "Thus saith the Lord!" The true prophet may be reluctant to speak out, but the fire in his breast compels him. His obedience to the divine prompting and his deep compassion will save him from the temptation of an ego trip. He will be willing to suffer in his own person for the stand he takes. Sometimes he will find it more than he can bear, but the divine prompting and the compassionate heart will spur him on.

Oscar Romero, when he became Archbishop of El Salvador, was a very unlikely candidate for this kind of ministry. He was considered a safe bet by the rich and the powerful in his land. By nature he was quiet, scholarly and conservative. The special grace in him was that he allowed himself to be transformed, to undergo a new conversion in the face of the profound injustice and suffering he saw around him. He, too, heard much "whispering", and there was terror on every side. Eventually he was martyred by an assassin's bullet while celebrating Mass in a convent.

In South Africa Archbishop Desmond Tutu emerged from the shadows of unwillingness to be, similarly, a prophetic figure. He stood in the gap when so many of the black political leaders were in prison or exile. With a passion like Romero's he proclaimed that the perpetrators of the evil of apartheid would without a shadow of doubt eventually "bite the dust", and all South Africans, black and white together, would be free. He was another who had to endure the "whispering" and hostility of many, even within his own church. Later, after the political transition had come, some of his opponents saw that he had been right, and they had to eat their words.

The prophet may at times have to face great inner pain and disillusionment. "Cursed be the day on which I was born!" complained Jeremiah (20:14). He endures and matures insofar as he puts his trust in God, even in great darkness. "The Lord is with me as a dread warrior ... they will not overcome me" (Jeremiah 20:11).

Thought for the day

"Offer thyself to God in a soft and tractable state, lest thou lose the impress of his fingers." (Irenaeus)

Prayer

Merciful God, strong and holy, grant to us all and especially to those in the front line of Christian witness, grace to hold on to the end.

Amen

Fifth Saturday in Lent
A betrayal of principle
Ez 37:21-28; Ps Jer 31:10-31; Jn 11:45-56

"It is expedient for you that one man should die for the people."

(John 11:50)

We are on the eve of Holy Week, when we watch with Jesus as he mounts his cross to accomplish the salvation of the world.

He was also caught up, humanly speaking, in the machinations of others. In our chosen verse for today we see, baldly stated, the dictates of expediency at work. The counsel of Caiaphas, the high priest, is full of irony. Jesus was to die not only for the Jewish nation but for all humankind, past, present and future. This was the meaning behind his final cry on the cross: "It is finished (accomplished)" (John 19:30). But Caiaphas saw it differently. The handing over of Jesus to the Roman authorities for execution would enable them as an occupied nation to save their skins.

Pontius Pilate also gave way to expediency. Knowing that he could find nothing in Jesus deserving of crucifixion, he nonetheless handed him over in order to appease the Jewish leaders and the crowd which they had stirred up. Jesus became the victim of sheer expediency, both Jewish and Gentile, taking this also to the cross and redeeming it with his prayer: "Father, forgive them, for they know not what they do."

Prudence is one thing, expediency is another. Expediency is a betrayal of principle. It is the soft option when we do not have the courage to take the harder, more costly way. Many boardrooms – political, industrial, commercial, agricultural, environmental and, yes, ecclesiastical – are probably encumbered with the concept and practice which goes "It is expedient that...." Refugees or asylum seekers: pollution and the ozone layer: ecumenical or inter-faith experiment: the role of women or children: the gulf between the developed and developing world: the war on terror.... "It is expedient that...."

What is needed is people of principle who are prepared to wrestle with different issues of right and wrong in any given situation, and to make choices based on these considerations, not on what is merely expedient. Christians need to discover and re-discover their vocation to follow this route, not arrogantly as if they have all the answers ready-made, but humbly, thoughtfully and purposefully in seeking to influence decisions made and options taken in the wider society.

Thought for the day

"How many times have I tried to wash my hands of the whole thing, but always that strange young man on his cross draws me back again."   (James Tyrell)

Prayer

Gracious and loving God, make us people of principle rather than expediency, of integrity rather than popularity, of justice and mercy rather than hardness of heart.

Amen

Clare Amos

Holy Week

Passion/Palm Sunday

Looking late in the day

Ps 118:1-2, 19-29; Mk 11:1-11

"He looked around at everything"

(Mark 11:11)

Theology is done through little phrases. It is the minor – apparently insignificant – differences between the gospel writers when they are seemingly telling us the same story that gives us a clue to their concerns. All four gospels tell us of the triumphal entry Jesus made into Jerusalem; all four also refer to a powerful gesture Jesus made in Jerusalem's temple (even though John's gospel locates this action near the beginning of Jesus' ministry rather than its end). But it is Mark alone who uses this short cryptic phrase, "He looked around at everything."

After his entry into the city he has gone to the temple. Matthew and Luke suggest that he set about cleansing it immediately. Not so Mark. In this gospel Jesus goes into the building for what reads almost like a military reconnaissance – but then withdraws again "as it was already late." He will come back the next morning – seeing a withered fig tree on his route – and then he will set about the task of dealing appropriately with this revered structure. We normally refer to the occasion as the "cleansing" the temple – though in fact it might be truer to say that Jesus was symbolically calling into question its very reason for existence. His actions will set in motion the train of events that would lead almost inexorably to his crucifixion. There is an ironic symmetry here. For his death will itself be marked by the rending in two of the temple veil – a clearly visible sign that this edifice had become redundant. God no longer had to be housed safe in a holy place, protected from intimate interrelationship with human beings, their lives and their deaths.

But for now he simply "looked around at everything". There is a sense of foreboding in this remark. It is "late", we are told, but is it simply late in the day – or also late in the time of God's forbearance with people? The incident with the figtree – withered and fruitless – strongly suggests that the divine patience is running out – and so he returns to the temple again, to turn things upside down, literally and figuratively.

If Jesus were to "look around at everything" in our world today what would he see? What emotions would it engender in him? Sadness? Anger? Compassion? What temples in our day and age still need to be cleansed – or even be told that their time is over? And just how late in the day is it already? Is the fig tree irrevocably withered – or can it still sprout new shoots to grow into God's tree of life?

Thought for the day
What would you be most ashamed of Jesus seeing if he looked around at everything in our world?

Prayer
Lord who looked,
Glance upon us even today.
We fear your eyes,
For they offer us both judgement and compassion.
Give us the strength to meet your gaze
and the confidence to look with you for what needs to be transformed in our world today.

Amen

Monday of Holy Week
No mean spirit
Is 42:1-7; Ps 26; Jn 12:1-11

"The house was filled with the fragrance."

(John 12:1-11)

Another evening, and a place not far away. And a woman whose gratitude and love refuses to allow itself to be means-tested. I have often thought of John's Gospel as a kind of love-story, in which through the chapters of the Gospel, the relationships between men and women which had gone so terribly wrong in Eden, are gradually restored to a life-giving balance and harmony – culminating in the new Eden, the meeting of Jesus and Mary in the garden of the resurrection (John 20). This story is a stage in that reworking of the relationship. We have already been told that Jesus unashamedly loved this woman – along with her sister and brother (John 11:5). Now we are to see the extravagance of her love in return. Her gesture scandalises – and not simply because of the costly 'waste' of the ointment that she uses. It has quite simply an erotic edge. And her passion seems actually to edge Jesus' own passion and death that much nearer. Passion and passion become strangely intermingled. It was always thus. The great saints and mystics, like Teresa of Avila and John of the Cross, knew that well. This woman has been granted the privilege by Jesus of matching the sheer extravagance and irrationality of his own love for humanity. At the core of our faith lies the costliest of self-giving. No measured means-testing in God's heart. That is the truth about this passage – rather than those Judas arguments about what is sensible and reasonable. Christians need to live dangerously or they do not live at all. This is not about not responding to the needs of the poor. For Jesus himself said that it was in meeting the needs of the poor that we would serve him. (Matthew 25:35-40). Rather it is suggesting that the pattern we should seek to live by – one in which we respond to Jesus – and those others in whom we see his face today – is not only in a spirit of justice but also with the exuberant and overflowing generosity of Mary.

Thought for the day

Jesus said, "The poor you will have always with you." Is this said as a statement of challenge or of judgement?

Prayer

Jesus, host and beloved guest,
help us not to measure meanly the love we bear for you.
Grant us a spirit of generosity,
So that we may be enabled to distinguish your features
In the kaleidoscope of our world's need.

Amen

Tuesday of Holy Week
The night of not yet
Is 49:1-6; Ps 70; Jn 13:21-33, 36-38

"You will follow afterwards"

(John 13:36)

The hour is later now. Before the end of this gospel passage it will become "night". In John's symbolic language "night" stands for the dark time when the forces of evil (and of lack of understanding) appear to have the ascendancy. So it is night as Judas the betrayer leaves the company to set about his terrible task.

But he is not the only disciple who still seems to be befogged. Peter too has things to learn. Indeed he even has to learn how much he has to learn. As always he seeks to run before he can walk, falls over and sticks his foot in his mouth in the process!

It seems strange that he should be told here that he "cannot follow ... now" (13:36). Was he not commanded to "follow Jesus" all those months or years ago on the shore of the Sea of Galilee? Was not that how the great adventure had begun? Not according to this Gospel. For while in Mark's Gospel Peter is summoned in this way as the first act of Jesus' public ministry, here in John's Gospel it is rather different. If you look carefully at the call of Peter in the first chapter of this Gospel, you find that the phrase "Follow me", is carefully, deliberately not used.

Others are commanded to "follow Jesus" – but not Peter. Peter is in fact first summoned by Jesus with those words only at the very end of the story, only after the resurrection. There – indeed by the shore of the Sea of Galilee – he mends the relationship which had been marred by his denial – and is rewarded both with a prediction of his own death and that final challenge "Follow me".

Peter cannot really, truly, deeply, follow Jesus until he knows about the dangerous path that Jesus will lead him on. That is what he is being told this night as Gethsemane approaches. Following Jesus must always be on the road that leads to and through the Cross – rather than seeks to bypass it.

Thought for the day

What can and does "following Jesus" on the Way of the Cross really mean in our society where Christianity is "safe" and prosperity is powerful?

Prayer

Light of the world,
You dispel the darkness, and banish the mists of despair.
Grant us the privilege of following you,
Even when we do not fully understand its awesome cost.

Amen

Wednesday of Holy Week
The Judas within
Is 50:4-9; Ps 68; Mt 26:14-25

"Surely not I, Rabbi?"

(Matthew 26:25)

It is paradoxical that the person we should read most about this week – other than Jesus himself – is Judas Iscariot. Judas has in fact featured in the Gospel readings for the previous two days as well as today. We will probably never know Judas' precise motivation for his actions – tradition has suggested financial greed, ambition or political disillusionment as possible reasons. But it is interesting just how much we want to distance Judas from ourselves – even Pilate, who after all had the ultimate power of life or death over Jesus, fares considerably better in Christian history. Judas is the figure we all love to hate and sadly the fact that his name was reminiscent of the word "Jew" was used to help justify the appalling centuries of Christian anti-semitism.

Perhaps even Judas himself could not quite bear or believe the role which was his. It is fascinating to reflect how different Bible translations can alter our perception of Judas – and even help us to realise that he may not be so far from the rest of us after all. Judas' response to Jesus' challenge has, in the original Greek, an ambiguity about it. Older translations pick up a note of hesitancy by using phrases such as "Could it be me?" By contrast the

New Revised Standard Version (NRSV)'s translation is a robust "Surely not I!" Does this change in emphasis somehow reflect the spirit of our age in which we seek, perhaps rather too often, to distance ourselves from responsibility for mistakes and wrongdoing? Are we all rather too keen on saying "Surely not I!" rather than confessing, "Could it be me?"?

It is right that Judas is so central to the story of Holy Week. It would be dangerous to banish him. But we need him to help us say "Could it be me", rather than insist, "Surely not I". There is a Judas within all of us that we need to acknowledge. Yet this is not the ultimate truth about ourselves. We also need to allow God's love to touch and heal our Judas selves – something that sadly it seems Judas himself could not quite bring himself to do. We need to learn that perhaps the most dangerous sin of all is refusing to face the enormity of God's love for us – whatever we have done.

Thought for the day

Are we people ourselves who more readily say "Could it be me?" or "Surely not I!"?

Prayer

(From an imaginative modern dialogue song by Cecily Taylor, in which Judas does finally assert the overwhelming love of God.)

Judas, Judas, where can we go
To bury our failures and aching woe?
No place; there's no place where we can hide
God's love stands waiting on every side.

Holy Thursday
Before the new beginning

Ex 12:8, 11-14; Ps 115; 1 Cor 11:3-26; Jn 13:1-15

"He loved them to the end."

(John 13:1)

Another evening, and another supper. According to John's chronology this took place five days after the meal at Bethany. Yet the echo of that earlier meal is too rarely registered. But just as then Mary had anointed Jesus' feet with oil, so now Jesus chooses to wash his disciples' feet with water. A strange congruence – dare we suggest that perhaps Jesus had even learned something from this woman about love and service? It is not the only similar congruence in this Gospel, for both Jesus and Mary weep and then suddenly discover a loved one standing before them raised from the dead. It seems almost as though this Gospel writer is suggesting one of the purposes of the life and ministry of Jesus is to restore the equilibrium in human relationships between male and female – unwinding the imbalance that had dominated human history since the days of Genesis.

But this new Genesis, new beginning, can only happen by an "end". With a typical Johannine double entendre, Jesus' actions at this meal are linked to the comment that "he loved them to the end" (John 13:1). The Gospel writer is wanting to tell us both that Jesus loved his disciples to the last moment of his life – and loved them to the ultimate.

Indeed the two senses are intricately connected for it was the supreme nature of Jesus' love for his friends that led him directly to the Cross, on which, of course, he spoke his final words, "It is finished" (John 19:30). Ends can be the source of new beginnings, as T S Eliot famously reminded us. And without these particular and definitive "ends" in the gospel story the evening of Holy Thursday will not be able to dawn into resurrection morning.

It is ironic, isn't it, that the gospels imply and church tradition firmly believes that it was only the male disciples of Jesus who were present that night he washed their feet? The woman whose extravagant gesture at Bethany had been a precursor of Jesus' own profligate love on this night is excluded. It will not be until a meeting in a garden on the other side of the "end" that love will speak to her again. Then the world can begin anew.

Thought for the day
Who do we seek to "exclude" from our sacred gatherings and inner circles? Why?

Prayer
God of ends and new beginnings,
Lord of supper places and gardens,
Encourage us to struggle for the ultimate:
for a love that is wide enough to embrace all
for a willingness to be the servant of all
and for a spirit of sacrifice that is prepared to offer its all.

Amen

Good Friday
Perfect moments
Is 52:13–53:12; Ps 30; Heb 4:14-16, 5: 7-9; Jn 18:1–19:42

"What I have written, I have written."

(John 19:22)

Running like a thread through Holy Week is a debate about power. It is there, menacingly, on Palm Sunday. It comes to its climax today on Good Friday. Particularly in the account of Jesus' passion given by the Gospel of John, the question is being teased out: where does true power really lie – with the representative of the greatest political authority of the time, or with an apparently vulnerable prisoner, a condemned member of one of Rome's subject nations? The verb "teased" is used deliberately – for what gives this Gospel's passion narrative its special strength are the savage ironies it employs to make this point. There is the purple robe, symbol of power, with which the soldiers dress Jesus. There is the glorious ambiguity in John 19:13 when it is impossible to decide whether the Greek text is stating that Pilate himself sat on the judge's bench – or sits Jesus there. Who indeed is on trial here, and who is the judge? And there is the inscription in all the key languages of that day and place that names "Jesus of Nazareth, the King of the Jews" which Pilate perversely refuses to alter when the objections of the religious leadership are pointed out to him. Even if he is saying more than he realises, his retort confirms the inscription – and validates it for all time.

When I teach New Testament Greek one of the features of the language I most enjoy exploring with students is the different tenses of verbs. The perfect tense in Greek is comparatively rare – and has a special significance. It is used to describe an action that has been completed – but whose consequence endures to the present. When Pilate responds 'What I have written, I have written' he uses a perfect verb. The gospel writer is by this means deliberately reminding us that what was said on an inscription over a condemned criminal in an outpost of the Roman empire circa 30^{AD} impacts on our present. It is still as true as it ever was. Despite all appearances to the contrary even today power rests with this man whose story seemed on the surface to speak of its opposite. His tale is quite literally one of naked power.

It is not the only "perfect moment" in the passion story. Jesus' own final word "It is finished" is itself a perfect verb. English translations can never seem quite to do justice to the richness of what is being said here, for Jesus is not simply uttering a sigh of relief that finally his suffering is over – but also proclaiming with a shout of triumph the goal and "completion" of his incarnate life and ministry – as well as asserting that its impact endures for eternity. In the whirlpool of our world today where great nations seem to be able to bend the vocabulary of justice and truth to fit their own definitions, we need this "perfect" assurance that the tense of the Word of God, glorious on his cruciform throne, will span the chasm of past, present and future.

Thought for the day

Do we really regard the passion of Christ as an event that impacts on our present, or do we emotionally and practically relegate it to the past?

Prayer

Word of God,
You speak to us most powerfully as you hang silent
on your cross,
Do not allow us to consign you to a moment
in past time,
But accomplish the purpose for which you
have been sent,
Creating a world where justice and truth can
reign for ever.

Amen

Holy Saturday
Delving deeper down

Rom 6:3-11

"By baptism into death."

(Romans 6:4)

One of the happiest days of my life was the time when my son was baptised. The day had, in one sense, been a long time coming. There had been several miscarriages, apparent infertility, some wearing and unsuccessful fertility treatment, a surprise (and completely natural!) pregnancy, precarious moments during both the second and third months, and finally a dose of pre-eclampsia which resulted in an emergency Caesarean and a premature baby. So we wanted to make our son's baptism, when he reached four months old, a day of real celebration and thanksgiving. It was a lovely service, held in St Martin's Church, Canterbury, a church which prides itself on being the oldest church in England in continuous use. It was an affirmation of life, this new and precious life which had been given to us to care for. Death seemed thankfully very far away.

It was not like that in the New Testament where baptism and death seem often to be intimately connected. In today's reading from Romans 6 we are reminded that though death is not the goal of baptism – it is an intrinsic part of it. A similar point is made in the conversation between Jesus and James and John when the two brothers are warned by Jesus to be prepared to be baptised with the baptism that Jesus himself experiences. The very practice of baptism in the early church – going down beneath the waters – was a visible reminder of this link, and of course choosing to make this act of commitment in the days before Constantine could often be the catalyst that led to persecution and death. It is an issue even today. A few months ago I was involved in a conference for church leaders who were ministering in Muslim-majority areas. One of the topics of discussion was the situation of "secret believers" – and whether it was appropriate in such circumstances for people always to be encouraged to undergo baptism. They were certainly aware of the real meaning of the rite!

It often seems to me that our understanding of Easter is a bit like our view of baptism – we are prepared to reflect on the sad and difficult aspects of the story on Good Friday – but then want to hurry along till Easter Sunday and put the doom and gloom firmly behind us. Our Easter services sometimes seem like an attempt to reverse Good Friday – rather than catch it up and transfigure it. In our western culture we seem to find it increasingly difficult to discover that the power of joy and sorrow comes from their strange intermingling. Perhaps people in other parts of the world where death still seems to be a more frequent visitor have important wisdom to share with us.

Thought for the day
Reflect for a few moments on what baptism symbolises to you. What kind of challenge does it offer you?

Prayer
Lord of creation,
Ruler of birth and death,
Give us the courage to delve more deeply into the mystery of faith.
For only then can we come to your true resurrection.

Amen

Easter Day
The unfinished sentence
Mk 16:1-7 (8)
"Going ahead of you."

(Mark 16:7)

This week's meditations began with several passages that were set in the "evening." They come to their conclusion, this Easter Day, with a biblical text that is very clearly set in the early morning. Resurrection and dawn go together. We have journeyed with Jesus "to the end" and through the night so we now have the joy of discovering a new beginning and a new day.

One of the particular features of the resurrection account in Mark's Gospel is its short, abrupt and even possibly unfinished quality. In fact in the second century AD it was felt to be so unfinished that some extra verses, 9-20, were added to round the story off properly. A key insight of biblical scholarship during the last 30 years or so has been the recognition that verse 8 is where Mark's Gospel ends – and where most likely he always intended his Gospel to end. Admittedly it certainly feels unfinished, in the Greek even more so than our English translations. The verse as it is written in Greek ends with the little word "gar" which means "for", which normally never ends a sentence, let alone a chapter or a book!

But that is exactly Mark's point. The resurrection is not about "ending" or coming to a full stop. Instead it offers the adventure of a new journey, a closer following of Jesus and a deeper awareness of the meaning of discipleship. The mysterious figure that the women meet at the tomb tells them that Jesus is going ahead of them to Galilee – which is of course their homeland. They are being offered the opportunity to meet the Risen Lord in the midst of their homes and everyday lives – and have them transfigured. Yet the journey in Mark's terms cannot end even there, for once they think they are settled in Galilee they will, metaphorically at least, be asked to journey with Jesus to Jerusalem once again, only this time being sure that they do not abandon him when danger threatens – instead travelling with him through the Cross to the resurrection.

The resurrection of Jesus does not mean that there is now nothing for us to do, no challenges to face, no difficulties to confront. Mark has deliberately allowed his Gospel to draw to its close with a sort of ellipsis ... the mark of an unfinished sentence. It is our task in our own lives and time to fill out the dots, and to begin to complete this sentence which knows no end.

Thought for the day

How can we – and CAFOD – help to complete this resurrection sentence today?

Prayer

Lord of the unfinished sentence,
The grammar of your resurrection is irregular,
Your syntax is demanding.
Help us to translate your language of love
Into the story of our own lives.

Amen